How Languages are Learned
Second edition

Also published in
Oxford Handbooks for Language Teachers

Teaching English Overseas: An Introduction
Sandra Lee McKay

Teaching American English Pronunciation
Peter Avery and Susan Ehrlich

Teaching Business English
Mark Ellis and Christine Johnson

Communication in the Language Classroom
Tony Lynch

Explaining English Grammar
George Yule

Teaching and Learning in the Language Classroom
Tricia Hedge

Doing Second Language Research
James Dean Brown and Theodore S. Rodgers

Teaching English as an International Language
Sandra Lee McKay

Intercultural Business Communication
Robert Gibson

How Languages are Learned

Second edition

Patsy M. Lightbown and Nina Spada

OXFORD
UNIVERSITY PRESS

OXFORD

UNIVERSITY PRESS

Great Clarendon Street, Oxford OX2 6DP

Oxford University Press is a department of the University of Oxford.
It furthers the University's objective of excellence in research, scholarship,
and education by publishing worldwide in

Oxford New York

Auckland Bangkok Buenos Aires Cape Town Chennai
Dar es Salaam Delhi Hong Kong Istanbul Karachi Kolkata
Kuala Lumpur Madrid Melbourne Mexico City Mumbai
Nairobi São Paulo Shanghai Taipei Tokyo Toronto

OXFORD and OXFORD ENGLISH are registered trade marks of
Oxford University Press in the UK and in certain other countries

ISBN 0 19 437000 3

Typeset in Adobe Garamond by Oxford University Press

Printed in China

To the teachers and students from whom
we have learned so much

CONTENTS

ACKNOWLEDGMENTS

Throughout the preparation of the second edition we have had the support and encouragement of many colleagues and students. Roy Lyster, Vicki Murphy, Laura Collins, Mela Sarkar, and Ahlem Ammar read chapters and offered valuable suggestions for improvement. Randall Halter was, as always, the rock solid man behind the computers. We appreciate the feedback offered by Henry Widdowson and two anonymous Oxford University Press reviewers.

We repeat our thanks to Leila Ranta and Jude Rand for their essential contributions to the first edition. We thank the English Speaking Union for conferring the 1993 Duke of Edinburgh book prize for Applied Linguistics on the book.

Above all, we are indebted to the many readers of the first edition. Without their enthusiastic response, which has astonished and delighted us, there would be no second edition!

The authors and publisher are grateful to those who have given permission to reproduce the following extracts and adaptations of copyright material:

Blackwell Publishers for permission to reproduce 'The sensitive period for the acquisition of syntax in a second language' by Mark Patkowski from *Language Learning* 30/2 (1980).

Cambridge University Press for permission to reproduce 'Constructing an acquisition-based procedure for second language assessment' by Pienemann, Johnson, and Brindley (1988) and 'Second language instruction does make a difference: Evidence from an empirical study of second language relativization' by Doughty from *Studies in Second Language Acquisition* 13/4 (1991).

Every effort has been made to trace the owners of copyright material in this book, but we should be pleased to hear from any copyright holder whom we have been unable to contact. We apologize for any apparent negligence. If notified, the publisher will be pleased to rectify any errors or omissions at the earliest opportunity.

Cartoons by Sophie Grillet © Oxford University Press 1993.

INTRODUCTION

Every few years, new foreign language teaching methods arrive on the scene. New textbooks appear far more frequently. They are usually proclaimed to be more effective than those that have gone before, and, in many cases, these methods or textbooks are promoted or even prescribed for immediate use. New methods and textbooks may reflect current developments in linguistic/applied linguistic theory or recent pedagogical trends. Sometimes they are said to be based on recent developments in language acquisition theory and research. For example, one approach to teaching may emphasize the value of having students imitate and practise a set of correct sentences while another emphasizes the importance of encouraging 'natural' communication between learners.

How is a teacher to evaluate the potential effectiveness of new methods? One important basis for this evaluation is, of course, the teacher's own experience with previous successes or disappointments. In addition, teachers who are informed about some of the findings of recent research are better prepared to judge whether the new proposals for language teaching are likely to bring about positive changes in students' learning.

This book about how languages are learned has been written for second and foreign language teachers. We believe that information about findings and theoretical views in second language acquisition research can help teachers evaluate claims made by textbook writers and proponents of various language teaching methods.

The book begins with a chapter on how children learn their first language. This background is important because both second language research and second language teaching have been influenced by changes in our understanding of how children acquire their first language. In fact, one of the significant findings of second language acquisition research has been that there are important similarities between first and second language acquisition. In Chapter 2, several theories which have been proposed to account for second language learning are presented and assessed. Questions raised in Chapters 1 and 2 include: What are some of the characteristics of language learning in the early stages? Is language learning just like any other kind of learning? To what extent can theories of first language acquisition be applied to second language learning? Is there a biologically determined age limit for language acquisition? How important are imitation and practice for language learning? Does it help to correct learners when they make errors?

In Chapter 3, we turn our attention to how individual learner characteristics and different contexts for second language learning may affect success. The discussion includes issues such as the importance of learners' attitudes toward the second language and its speakers, and the possibility that there is a special aptitude for language learning. The question of how the learner's age affects success in second language learning is also discussed.

In Chapter 4, we review some of the research findings about second language learners' changing knowledge of the language and their ability to use that knowledge. We look at interpretations of learners' errors and at the characteristics of learners' language at different stages of development.

Chapter 5 begins with a comparison of natural and instructional environments for second language learning. We then examine some different ways in which classroom researchers have observed and described teaching practices in second language classrooms. Transcriptions of teacher–student interactions illustrate some of the ways in which language learning in the classroom may be affected by the special characteristics of that environment.

In Chapter 6, we examine five proposals for the most effective way to teach a second language. For each of the proposals, research findings are presented and discussed. This makes it possible to reflect on the type and amount of evidence available for assessing the effectiveness of the different approaches.

In Chapter 7, some popular views about language learning and teaching are critically examined in light of current research.

A Glossary provides a quick reference for a number of terms which may be new or which have specific technical meanings in the context of language acquisition research. Glossary words are italicized where they first appear in the text. For readers who would like to have more detailed information about some of the research, a list of sources and further readings is included at the end of each chapter, and there is a Bibliography at the end of the book.

We have tried to present the information in a way which does not assume that readers are already familiar with research methods or theoretical issues. Each chapter summarizes important developments in first and/or second language acquisition research and theory. Examples and case studies are included throughout the book to illustrate the research ideas. Many of the examples are taken from second language classrooms. We have included a number of activities which give readers the opportunity to practise some of the techniques of observation and analysis from which we have drawn the ideas presented in this book.

1   Languages are learned mainly through imitation.

strongly agree _____|____|____|____|____|_____ strongly disagree

2   Parents usually correct young children when they make grammatical errors.

strongly agree _____|____|____|____|____|_____ strongly disagree

3   People with high IQs are good language learners.

strongly agree _____|____|____|____|____|_____ strongly disagree

4   The most important factor in second language acquisition success is motivation.

strongly agree _____|____|____|____|____|_____ strongly disagree

5   The earlier a second language is introduced in school programs, the greater the likelihood of success in learning.

strongly agree _____|____|____|____|____|_____ strongly disagree

6   Most of the mistakes which second language learners make are due to interference from their first language.

strongly agree _____|____|____|____|____|_____ strongly disagree

7   Teachers should present grammatical rules one at a time, and learners should practise examples of each one before going on to another.

strongly agree _____|____|____|____|____|_____ strongly disagree

8   Teachers should teach simple language structures before complex ones.

strongly agree _____|____|____|____|____|_____ strongly disagree

9   Learners' errors should be corrected as soon as they are made in order to prevent the formation of bad habits.

strongly agree _____|____|____|____|____|_____ strongly disagree

10 Teachers should use materials that expose students to only those language structures which they have already been taught.

strongly agree _____|____|____|____|____|_____ strongly disagree

11 When learners are allowed to interact freely (for example in group or pair activities), they learn each others' mistakes.

strongly agree _____|____|____|____|____|_____ strongly disagree

12 Students learn what they are taught.

strongly agree _____|____|____|____|____|_____ strongly disagree

Before we begin . . .

It is probably true, as some have claimed, that most of us teach as we were taught or in a way that reflects our ideas and preferences about learning. Take a moment to reflect on your views about how languages are learned and what the implications are for how they should be taught. On page xv are twelve popular views about language learning. Think about whether you agree or disagree with some of these views. Complete the questionnaire and keep these ideas in mind as you read about current research and theory in second language learning.

In the last chapter of this book, we will return to these popular views and examine them in the light of the research on language learning which is discussed in Chapters 1–6.

1 LEARNING A FIRST LANGUAGE

Language acquisition is one of the most impressive and fascinating aspects of human development. We listen with pleasure to the 'coos' and 'gurgles' of a three-month-old baby. We laugh and 'answer' the conversational 'ba-ba-ba' babbling of older babies, and we share in the pride and joy of parents whose one-year-old has uttered the first 'bye-bye'. Indeed, learning a language is an amazing feat—one which has attracted the attention of linguists and psychologists for generations. How do children accomplish this? What is it that enables a child not only to learn words, but to put them together in meaningful sentences? What pushes children to go on developing complex grammatical language even though their early simple communication is successful for most purposes?

In this chapter, we will look briefly at some of the characteristics of the language of young children. We will then consider several theories which have been offered as explanations for how language is learned.

Milestones and patterns in development

One remarkable thing about first language acquisition is the high degree of similarity which we see in the early language of children all over the world. The earliest vocalizations are simply the involuntary crying that babies do when they are hungry or uncomfortable. Soon, however, we hear the cooing and gurgling sounds of contented babies, lying in their beds looking at bright shapes and colours around them. Even in these early weeks and months of life, however, infants are able to hear very subtle differences between the sounds of human language. In cleverly designed experiments, scientists have been able to show that tiny babies can hear the difference between 'pa' and 'ba', for example. And yet, it will be many months before their own vocalizations (babbling) begin to reflect the characteristics of the different languages they are learning.

By the end of their first year, most babies understand quite a few frequently repeated words. They wave when someone says 'bye-bye'; they clap when someone says 'pat-a-cake'; they eagerly hurry to the kitchen when 'juice and cookies' are announced. At 12 months, most babies will have begun to produce a word or two that everyone recognizes. From this time on, the number of words they understand and produce grows rapidly. By the age of two, most children reliably produce at least fifty different words and some produce many many more. About this time, they begin to combine words into simple sentences such as 'Mommy juice' and 'baby fall down'. These sentences are sometimes called 'telegraphic' because they often leave out such things as articles, prepositions, and auxiliary verbs. We recognize them as sentences because, even though function words and *grammatical morphemes* are missing, the word order reflects the word order of the language they are hearing and the combined words have a meaning relationship between them which makes them more than just a list of words. Thus, for an English-speaking child, 'kiss baby' does not mean the same thing as 'baby kiss'. Remarkably, we also see evidence, even in these early sentences, that children are doing more than imperfectly imitating what they have heard. Their two- and three-word sentences show signs that they are creatively combining words: 'more outside' in a situation where the meaning seems to be 'I want to go outside again' or 'Daddy uh-oh' which seems to mean 'Daddy fell down'.

By the age of three-and-a-half or four years, most children can ask questions, give commands, report real events, and create stories about imaginary ones—complete with correct grammatical morphemes. In fact, it is generally accepted that by age four, children have mastered the basic structures of the language or languages which have been spoken to them in these early years. In addition to the evidence we have from simply talking and listening to children, some carefully designed procedures have been developed to explore children's knowledge of language. One of the best known is the so-called 'wug test' developed by Jean Berko Gleason. In this 'test', children are shown pictures of imaginary creatures with novel names or people performing mysterious actions. For example, they are told, 'Here is a wug. Now there are two of them. There are two ___.' or 'Here is a man who knows how to bod. Yesterday he did the same thing. Yesterday, he ___.' By completing these sentences with 'wugs' and 'bodded', children demonstrate that they actually know the rules for the formation of plural and simple past in English, not just a list of memorized word pairs such as 'book/books' and 'nod/nodded', and can apply these rules to words which they have never heard before.

Children's ability to understand language and to use it to express themselves develops rapidly in the pre-school years. *Metalinguistic awareness*—the ability to treat language as an object, separate from the meaning it conveys—develops more slowly. A dramatic development in metalinguistic awareness occurs when children begin to learn to read. Although metalinguistic awareness begins to develop well before this time, seeing words represented by letters on a page leads children to a new level of awareness of language as separate from the meaning it represents. Three-year-old children can tell you that it's 'wrong' to say 'drink the chair', but while they would never say 'cake the eat' they will not be able to say what is wrong with it. A five-year-old on the other hand, knows that 'drink the chair' is silly in a different way from 'cake the eat'. Unlike a three-year-old, a child who can read comes to understand that 'caterpillar' is a longer word than 'train' even though the object it represents is substantially shorter! Metalinguistic awareness also includes the discovery of such things as ambiguity—words and sentences that have multiple meaning. This gives children access to word jokes, trick questions, and riddles which they love to share with their friends and family.

Early childhood bilingualism

Many children, perhaps the majority of children in the world, are exposed to more than one language in early childhood. Children who hear more than one language virtually from birth are sometimes referred to as 'simultaneous bilinguals', whereas those who begin to learn a *second language* later are referred to as 'sequential bilinguals'. There is a considerable body of research on the ability of young children to learn more than one language in their earliest years. The evidence suggests that, when simultaneous bilinguals are in contact with both languages in a variety of settings, there is every reason to expect that they will progress in their development of both languages at a rate and in a manner which are not different from those of monolingual children. Naturally, when children go on to have schooling in only one of those languages, there may be considerable differences in the amount of metalinguistic knowledge they develop and in the type and extent of the vocabulary they eventually acquire in the two languages. Nevertheless, there seems to be little support for the myth that learning more than one language in early childhood slows down the child's linguistic or cognitive development.

There may be reason to be concerned, however, about situations where children are virtually cut off from their family language when they are 'submerged' in a second language for long periods in early schooling or day care. In such cases, children may begin to lose the family language before they have developed an age-appropriate mastery of the new language. This is referred to as *subtractive bilingualism*, and it can have serious negative consequences for children from minority groups. In some cases, children seem to continue to be caught between two languages: not having mastered the second language, they have not continued to develop the first. Unfortunately, the 'solution' which educators often propose to parents is that they should stop speaking the family language at home and concentrate instead on speaking the majority language with their children. The evidence seems to suggest that the opposite would be more effective. That is, parents who themselves are learners of the majority language should continue to use the language which is most comfortable for them. The children may eventually prefer to answer in the majority language, but at least they will maintain their comprehension of their family language. This also permits the parents to express their knowledge and ideas in ways that are likely to be richer and more elaborate than they can manage in their second language.

There is no evidence that a child's brain has a limited capacity for languages such that their knowledge of one language must shrink if their knowledge of the other one grows. Most minority language children do eventually master the majority language, but second language acquisition takes time. It may take several years for children to know the language well enough to use it for school learning with the same ease as children who have learned the language from birth. Eventually, however, it is likely to become their preferred language. Demographic research shows that minority languages are usually lost in the second generation after immigration. Children who have the opportunity to learn multiple languages from early childhood and to maintain them throughout their lives are fortunate indeed, and families that can offer this opportunity to their children should be encouraged to do so.

Developmental sequences

As children progress through the discovery of language in their early years, there are predictable patterns in the emergence and development of many features of the language they are learning. For some of these features, these patterns have been described in terms of *developmental sequences* or 'stages'. To some extent, these stages in language acquisition are related to children's cognitive development. For example, children do not use temporal adverbs such as 'tomorrow' or 'last week' correctly until they develop an adequate understanding of time. In other cases, the developmental sequences seem to be determined more by the gradual mastery of the linguistic elements for expressing ideas which have been present in children's cognitive understanding for a long time.

Grammatical morphemes

Much research has focused on how children develop grammatical morphemes in English. One of the best-known studies of this development in child first language development was carried out by Roger Brown and his colleagues in the 1960s. He studied the development of three children (whom he called Adam, Eve, and Sarah) whose mother tongue was English. One aspect of the research was how the children acquired 14 grammatical morphemes over time. He found that they acquired them in a remarkably similar sequence (Brown 1973). Below is a partial list of the grammatical morphemes studied by Roger Brown, in the approximate order of their acquisition by Adam, Eve, and Sarah.

> present progressive *-ing* (Mommy runn*ing*)
> plural *-s* (two book*s*)
> irregular past forms (Baby *went*)
> possessive *'s* (daddy*'s* hat)
> copula (Annie *is* a nice girl)
> articles 'the' and 'a'
> regular past *-ed* (She walk*ed*)
> third person singular simple present *-s* (She run*s*)
> auxiliary 'be' (He *is* coming)

A child who had mastered the grammatical morphemes at the bottom of the list was sure to have mastered those at the top, but the reverse was not true. Thus, Brown could claim there was evidence for a developmental sequence or *order of acquisition*. The children did not master the morphemes at the same *rate,* however. For example, Eve had mastered nearly all the morphemes before she was two-and-a-half years old while Sarah and Adam were still working on them when they were three-and-a-half or four. The study carried out by Brown was a *longitudinal* study, that is, he studied the same learners over an extended period of time.

In other first language research on morpheme acquisition, Jill and Peter de Villiers did a *cross-sectional* study (1973). They studied 21 children who were at different ages and stages of development. They found that children who correctly used the morphemes which Adam, Eve, and Sarah had acquired late were also correct in using the ones which Adam, Eve, and Sarah had acquired earlier. Those children who accurately used the 'early' morphemes, however, had not necessarily mastered the 'late' ones. The children mastered the morphemes at different ages, just as Adam, Eve, and Sarah had done, but again the *order* of their acquisition was very similar. They were similar to each other *and* similar to Adam, Eve, and Sarah.

Negation

Lois Bloom's longitudinal study of three children, Kathryn, Gia, and Eric, included a detailed analysis of the development of negation when they were less than three years old. The children learned the functions of negation very early. That is, they learned to deny, reject, disagree with, and refuse something. However, even though they had this awareness of how negation functions, it took some time before they learned the grammatical rules to express these negative functions (see Bloom and Lahey 1978). The following stages in the development of negation have been observed.

Stage 1

The child's first negatives are usually expressed by the word 'no', either all alone or as the first word in the utterance.

> No go. No cookie. No comb hair.

Some children even adopt the word 'any' as a negator, perhaps with an accompanying shake of the head.

> Any bath!

Stage 2

As utterances grow longer, and the sentence subject is included, the negative usually appears just before the verb:

> Daddy no comb hair.

Stage 3

At this stage, the negative element is inserted into a more complex sentence. Children may add forms of the negative other than *no*, including words like '*can't*' and '*don't*'. These sentences appear to follow the correct English pattern of attaching the negative to the auxiliary or modal verb. However, the negative words do not yet vary these forms for different persons or tenses:

> I can't do it. He don't want it.

Stage 4

Later, children begin to attach the negative element to the correct form of auxiliary verbs such as 'do' and 'be', and modal verbs such as 'can':

> You didn't have supper. She doesn't want it.

They may still have difficulty with some other features related to negatives.

> I don't have no more candies.

Questions

There is a remarkable consistency as well in the way children learn to form questions in English. For one thing, there is a predictable order in which the '*wh-* words' emerge (for more details see Bloom and Lahey 1978).

'What' is generally the first *wh-* question word to be used. It is often learned as part of a whole ('Whatsat?' or 'Whatsit?') and it is some time before the child learns that there are variations of the form, such as 'What is that?' and 'What are these?'

'Where' and 'who' emerge very soon, reflecting the fact that the child can generally ask questions that they can already answer, questions about the here and now. This is reinforced by the fact that adults tend to ask children just these types of questions in the early days of language learning.

'Why' emerges around the end of the second year and becomes a favourite for the next year or two! Children seem to ask an endless number of questions beginning with 'why'. At this age, the child does not always seem to have a very good understanding of the meaning of the word, but has clearly discovered the usefulness of this little word in getting adults to engage in conversation.

Finally, when the child begins to understand manner and time, 'how' and 'when' emerge. In contrast to 'what', 'where', and 'who' questions, children sometimes ask the more cognitively difficult 'why', 'when', and 'how' questions without fully understanding their meaning, as the following conversation with a four-year-old clearly shows:

> **Child** When can we go outside?
> **Parent** In about five minutes.
> **Child** 1-2-3-4-5!! Can we go now?

Since the ability to use these question words is at least partly tied to children's cognitive development and to the types of questions which children are asked, it is perhaps not surprising that there is consistency in the sequence of their acquisition. Perhaps more remarkable is the consistency in the acquisition of word order in questions. This development is not based on learning new meanings, but rather on learning different linguistic forms to express meanings which are already clear—both to the child and to the interlocutor.

Stage 1
Children's earliest questions are single words or simple two- or three-word sentences with rising intonation:

> Cookie? Mommy book?

At the same time, of course, they may produce some correct questions— correct because they have been learned as *formulaic* 'chunks':

> Where's Daddy? What's that?

Stage 2
When their sentences grow longer, and they begin to ask more new questions, children use the word order of the declarative sentence. With 'yes/no' questions, they simply add rising intonation. With *wh-* questions, they put a question word at the beginning:

> You like this? I have some? Why you catch it?

At this stage, they may continue to produce the correct 'chunk-learned' forms such as 'What's that?' alongside their own created questions.

Stage 3
Gradually, they notice that the structure of questions is different and begin to produce questions such as:

> Can I go? Is that mine?

But at this stage they may generalize that all questions are formed by putting a verb at the beginning of a sentence. Thus:

> Is the teddy is tired? Do I can have a cookie?

Furthermore, at this stage, *wh-* questions usually retain the declarative word order:

> Why you don't have one?

The children seem to have worked out that, in a question, some element must appear at the beginning of the sentence, but they are not yet aware that there must also be some change in the internal word order of the sentence itself. We can call this stage 'fronting', because the children place some sort of question marker—an auxiliary verb or a *wh-* word—at the front of the sentence, but they do not yet change the order of the elements within the sentence.

Stage 4

Later, children begin to use subject–auxiliary inversion and can even add 'do' in sentences in which there would be no auxiliary in the declarative version of the sentence:

> Do you like ice cream?

Even at this stage, however, it sometimes seems that they can either use inversion or use a *wh-* word, but not both. Therefore, we may find inversion in 'yes/no' questions but not in *wh-* questions, except formulas such as 'What's that?' which may still be used:

> Can he eat the cookie? Where I can draw them?

Stage 5

Eventually, children combine both operations:

> Why can he go out?

However, it may still be beyond their ability to carry out a third or fourth operation, for example to negate the question as well as invert it:

> Why he can't go out?

Stage 6

Finally, when performance on questions is correct and well established, there is still one more hurdle. When *wh-* words appear in subordinate clauses or embedded questions, children overgeneralize the inverted form and produce sentences such as:

> I don't know why can't he go out.

By the age of four, most English speaking children have passed through these developmental stages and ask questions that are both grammatical and appropriate. This does not mean that they never slip back to an earlier stage. Overall, however, their speech shows that they have acquired this part of their language.

Summary

These descriptions of early milestones and acquisition sequences for grammatical morphemes, negatives, and questions show that we have considerable knowledge of *what* children learn in their early language development. More controversial, however, are questions about *how* this remarkable development takes place. Over the past fifty years, there have been three main theoretical approaches to explaining it: behaviourist, innatist, and interactionist approaches.

Theoretical approaches to explaining first language learning

Behaviourism: Say what I say

Behaviourism is a psychological theory of learning which was very influential in the 1940s and 1950s, especially in the United States. Traditional behaviourists believed that *language learning* is the result of imitation, practice, feedback on success, and habit formation. Children imitate the sounds and patterns which they hear around them and receive positive reinforcement (which could take the form of praise or just successful communication) for doing so. Thus encouraged by their environment, they continue to imitate and practise these sounds and patterns until they form 'habits' of correct language use. According to this view, the quality and quantity of the language which the child hears, as well as the consistency of the reinforcement offered by others in the environment, should have an effect on the child's success in language learning.

The behaviourist view of how language is learned has an intuitive appeal. And there is no doubt that it can offer a partial explanation of some aspects of children's early language learning. However, it is useful to examine actual language data to see how well this view accounts for the development of some more complex aspects of their language.

The behaviourists view imitation and practice as primary processes in language development. To clarify what is meant by these two terms, consider the following definitions and examples.

Imitation: Word-for-word repetition of all or part of someone else's utterance.

> **Mother** Would you like some bread and peanut butter?
> **Katie**   Some bread and peanut butter.

Practice: Repetitive manipulation of form.

> **Michel** I can handle it. Hannah can handle it. We can handle it.

Activity

Analysing children's speech

Examine these transcripts from Peter, Cindy, and Kathryn, who are about the same age. The transcripts are based on recordings made while the children were playing with a visiting adult. Look for examples of imitation and practice.

Transcription conventions:

xxx = incomprehensible speech

. . . = pause

parentheses = description of non-verbal events

Peter (24 months)
(Peter is playing with a dump truck while two adults, Patsy and Lois, look on.)

> **Peter** Get more.
> **Lois**   You're gonna put more wheels in the dump truck?
> **Peter** Dump truck. Wheels. Dump truck.

(later)

> **Patsy** What happened to it (the truck)?
> **Peter** (looking under chair for it) Lose it. Dump truck! Dump truck! Fall! Fall!
> **Lois**   Yes, the dump truck fell down.
> **Peter** Dump truck fell down. Dump truck.

Peter (25 months)
(Peter, Patsy, and Lois are playing with pencil and paper.)

> **Peter** (indicating he wants Patsy to draw) Lois. Lois too. Patsy. Lois too!
> **Patsy** You want me to make a car? OK.

(Patsy draws a tiny car like Lois's.)

> **Patsy** Oh, you want Lois to have some paper?
> **Peter** Lois have some paper?

(later)

> **Patsy** Let's see if I can draw what you draw. Draw something!

Peter Draw something!
(Unpublished data from P. M. Lightbown)

It is easy to see that Peter imitates a great deal. However, it should be stressed that not all children imitate to the extent that Peter does. Some 30–40 per cent of Peter's speech consists of imitations while, for some children, the rate of imitation may be less than 10 per cent.

It is also important to note that children's imitations are not random; they don't imitate everything they hear. Very detailed analyses showed that Peter imitated new words and sentence structures until they became solidly grounded in his language system, and then he stopped imitating these and went on to imitate other new words and structures. Thus, unlike a parrot who imitates the familiar and continues to repeat the same things again and again, children's imitation is selective and based on what they are currently learning. In other words, even when the child imitates, the choice of what to imitate seems to be based on something the child has already begun to understand, not simply on what is 'available' in the environment.

Cindy (24 months, 16 days)
(Cindy is looking at a picture of a carrot in a book and trying to get Patsy's attention.)

> **Cindy** Kawo? kawo? kawo? kawo? kawo?
> **Patsy** What are the rabbits eating?
> **Cindy** They eating . . . kando?
> **Patsy** No, that's a carrot.
> **Cindy** Carrot. (pointing to each carrot on the page) The other . . .
> carrot. The other carrot. The other carrot.

(A few minutes later, Cindy brings Patsy a stuffed toy rabbit.)

> **Patsy** What does this rabbit like to eat?
> **Cindy** (xxx) eat the carrots.

(Cindy gets another stuffed rabbit.)

> **Cindy** He (xxx) eat carrots. The other one eat carrots. They both eat
> carrots.

(One week later, Cindy opens the book to the same page.)

> **Cindy** Here's the carrots. (pointing) Is that a carrot?
> **Patsy** Yes.

Cindy (25 months, 1 day)

> **Cindy** (playing with several dolls, one of which she calls a 'tiger') Doll
> go to sleep.
> **Patsy** Does the doll want to go to sleep?

> **Cindy** (not answering Patsy, but talking to dolls in 'motherly' tones) Okay, I take you. Come on, Doll . . . (xxx). Go to sleep with the tiger (xxx) go to sleep. Doll wants to go to sleep.
> **Patsy** Does the tiger want to go to sleep?
> **Cindy** Tiger wants to go to sleep. The doll wants to go to sleep. He go to sleep.

(Unpublished data from P. M. Lightbown)

Cindy appears to be working hard on her language acquisition. She practises new structures in a way that sometimes makes her sound like a student in a foreign language classroom! Her 'He eat carrots. The other one eat carrots. They both eat carrots' is reminiscent of a *substitution drill*. However, again it should be stressed that not all children 'practise' to the extent that Cindy does in these examples, and Cindy herself is practising more here than in some other samples of her speech. Most important, it's Cindy who has chosen what she will imitate and practise.

The samples of speech from Peter and Cindy would seem to lend some support to the behaviourist explanation of language acquisition. But such imitation and practice do not account for how these children learn all aspects of their native language. Furthermore, we also need to account for the normal language development of children who rarely imitate and practise in the way that Peter and Cindy do in these examples. Look for examples of imitation and practice in the following conversation between Kathryn and Lois. Who is in charge of this conversation?

Kathryn (24 months)

> **Lois** Did you see the toys I brought?
> **Kathryn** I bring toys? Choo choo? Lois brought the choo choo train?
> **Lois** Yes, Lois brought the choo choo train.
> **Kathryn** (reaching for bag) I want play with choo choo train. I want play with choo choo train. (taking out slide) Want play. What's this?
> **Lois** Oh you know what that is.
> **Kathryn** Put down on floor. This. I do this.

(Kathryn puts the slide on the floor.)

> **Kathryn** (taking out two cars of train) Do this. I want do this. (trying to put train together) I do this. I do this.
> **Lois** OK. You can do it. You can do it. Look I'll show you how.

(Lois puts it together.)

> **Kathryn** (searching in box) I get more. Get a more. No more choo choo train. Get truck. (taking out truck) Kathryn truck. Where? Where a more choo choo train?

> **Lois**   Inside. It's in the box.
> **Kathryn** A choo choo? (taking out part of train) This is a choo choo
>   train.

(Bloom and Lahey 1978)

Like Cindy, Kathryn sometimes repeats herself or produces a series of related 'practice' sentences but rarely imitates the other speaker. Instead, she answers questions or poses them. She also elaborates on the other speaker's questions or statements. She is very much in charge of the conversation and the activity here!

Other children

Look at the following examples taken from various children in which imitation does not appear to be involved. Think about how the children arrive at the forms they produce. (These examples are from unpublished data collected by P. M. Lightbown and J. Rand.)

(Note: The ages of children are shown in years and months: for example, 6,10 means six years and ten months.)

1 **Kyo** (6,10) I'm hungry.
   Dad   We'll have some poppy seed bread in a little while.
   Kyo   No. I want it now.
   Dad   We have to wait 'til it's defrosted.
   Kyo   But I like it *frossed*.

2 Randall had a little bump on his hand and his mother said that they'd have to take him to the doctor.

   Randall (3,0) Why? So he can *doc* my little bump?

3 **Michel** (2,10) Mummy, I'm *hiccing up* and I can't stop.

4 **Mother**   Get undressed (after many repetitions)
   David (3,11) I'm getting undressed.
                    I'm getting *on dressed*.
                    I'm getting on dressed.
                    I'm getting *off dressed*.

Numbers 1–4 are all examples of children in the process of learning the rules of word formation and overgeneralizing them to new contexts.

(1) Kyo recognizes the prefix *de-* as negating the root word, so his version of the opposite of 'defrosted' comes out as 'frossed'.

(2) Randall forms the verb 'doc' from the noun 'doctor', by analogy with farmers who farm, swimmers who swim, and actors who act.

(3) Michel has heard many two-word verbs with *up*, such as 'standing up' and 'picking up'. On that basis, his generalization is perfectly sensible.

(4) David isn't sure what he hears. He doesn't yet understand the prefix *un-*. After repeating what he has heard, he analyses the sounds and concludes that it is 'on dressed'. Then he analyses the situation and concludes that this time he's supposed to be taking things *off* and so he arrives at the conclusion that he should be getting 'off dressed', not 'on dressed'.

5 At Lucy's twelfth birthday party, toasts were proposed with grape juice in stemmed glasses:

Father   I'd like to propose a toast.

After a long period without toasts, David raised his glass:

David (5,1) I'd like to propose a piece of bread.

Only after all the laughter sent David slinking from the table did the group realize that he wasn't joking!

6   **Mother**   I love you to pieces.
      David (4,1) I love you *three* pieces.

Numbers 5 and 6 are examples of a child in the process of discovering the full (or limited) meaning of the word in question.

(5) David is fascinated by the ritual language which accompanies this strange new event of lifting glasses. He is concentrating so hard on performing the gesture and the formulaic expression 'I'd like to propose …' that he fails to realize that the word he already knows—'toast'—is not the same toast and can't be replaced with a phrase which is its near-synonym in other contexts—a piece of bread.

(6) What does 'to pieces' mean anyway? At least *two* pieces would give some indication of how much she loves me! So David increases the quantity of love: Three pieces!

7 **Randall** (2,9) Are dogs can wiggle their tails?

8 **Randall** (3,5) You took all the towels away because I can't dry my hands.

Numbers 7 and 8 are both examples of systematic misuse of basic sentence construction which has not been fully acquired.

(7) Randall is in stage 3 of question formation. He has concluded that the trick of asking questions is to put a certain word at the beginning of the sentence—somewhat like the French *est-ce que* form. Other examples from this stage in his development include 'Are those are my boots?' and 'Are this is hot?'

(8) He means 'I can't dry my hands because you took all the towels away'. He has made a mistake about which clause comes first. Children at this age tend to state events in the order of their occurrence. In this case, the towels

disappeared before Randall attempted to dry his hands, so that's what he says first. He doesn't understand how a word like 'before' or 'because' can change that order around.

These examples of children's speech provide us with a window on the process of language learning. Imitation and practice alone cannot explain some of the forms created by the children. They are not sentences that they heard from adults. Rather, children appear to pick out patterns and then generalize them to new contexts. They create new forms or new uses of words until they finally figure out how the forms are used by adults. Their new sentences are usually comprehensible and often correct.

The behaviourist explanations for language acquisition offer a reasonable way of understanding how children learn some of the regular and routine aspects of language. However, their acquisition of the more complex grammatical structures of the language requires a different sort of explanation and we will see below some of the proposals for going beyond imitation and practice.

Innatism: It's all in your mind

The linguist Noam Chomsky claims that children are biologically programmed for language and that language develops in the child in just the same way that other biological functions develop. For example, every child will learn to walk as long as adequate nourishment and reasonable freedom of movement are provided. The child does not have to be taught. Most children learn to walk at about the same age, and walking is essentially the same in all normal human beings. For Chomsky, language acquisition is very similar. The environment makes a basic contribution—in this case, the availability of people who speak to the child. The child, or rather, the child's biological endowment, will do the rest. This is known as the innatist position. Chomsky proposed his theory in reaction to what he saw as the inadequacy of the behaviourist theory of learning based on imitation and habit formation (Chomsky 1959).

Chomsky argues that the behaviourist theory fails to recognize what has come to be called 'the logical problem of language acquisition'. This logical problem refers to the fact that children come to know more about the structure of their language than they could reasonably be expected to learn on the basis of the samples of language which they hear. According to Chomsky, the language the child is exposed to in the environment is full of confusing information (for example, false starts, incomplete sentences, or slips of the tongue) and does not provide all the information which the child needs. Furthermore, the evidence seems very strong that children are by no means systematically corrected or instructed on language. Parental corrections of language errors have been observed to be inconsistent or even non-existent for children of pre-school age. When parents do correct, they tend to focus on meaning and not on language form, often simply repeating the child's incorrect utterance in a more complete grammatical form. When parents do correct errors, children often ignore the correction, continuing to use their own ways of saying things.

According to Chomsky, children's minds are not blank slates to be filled merely by imitating language they hear in the environment. Instead he claims that children are born with a special ability to discover for themselves the underlying rules of a language system.

Chomsky originally referred to this special ability as a *language acquisition device* (LAD). This device was often described as an imaginary 'black box' which exists somewhere in the brain. This 'black box', thought to contain all and *only* the principles which are universal to all human languages, prevents the child from going off on lots of wrong trails in trying to discover the rules of the language. For the LAD to work, the child needs access only to samples of a natural language. These language samples serve as a trigger to activate the device. Once it is activated, the child is able to discover the structure of the language to be learned by matching the innate knowledge of basic grammatical relationships to the structures of the particular language in the environment. In recent writings, Chomsky and his followers no longer use the term LAD, but refer to the child's innate endowment as *Universal Grammar* (UG). UG is considered to consist of a set of principles which are common to all languages. If children are pre-equipped with UG, then what they have to learn is the ways in which their own language makes use of these principles and the variations on those principles which may exist in the particular language which they hear spoken around them (Chomsky 1981, Cook 1988, White 1989).

Chomsky drew attention to the fact that children seem to develop language in similar ways and on a similar schedule, in a way not very different from the way all children learn to walk. Environmental differences may be associated with some variation in the rate of acquisition (how quickly children learn), but adult linguistic *competence* (the knowledge of how their language works) is very similar for all speakers of one dialect or language. In acquiring the intricate and complex systems that make up a language, young children, whose cognitive abilities are fairly limited in many ways, accomplish something which adult second language learners may envy.

Here is a summary of the kinds of evidence which have been used to support Chomsky's innatist position:

1   Virtually all children successfully learn their native language at a time in life when they would not be expected to learn anything else so complicated. Children who are profoundly deaf will learn sign language if they are exposed to it in infancy, and their progress in language acquisition is similar to that of hearing children. Even children with very limited cognitive ability develop quite complex language systems if they are brought up in environments in which people talk to them and engage them in communication.

2   Children successfully master the basic structure of their native language or dialect in a variety of conditions: some which would be expected to enhance language development (for example, caring, attentive parents who focus on the child's language), and some which might be expected to inhibit it (for example, abusive or rejecting parents). Children achieve different levels of vocabulary, creativity, social grace, and so on, but virtually all achieve mastery of the structure of the language spoken around them. This is seen as support for the hypothesis that language is somehow separate from other aspects of cognitive development and may even be located in a different part of the brain. The term 'modular' is sometimes used to represent the notion that the brain has different 'modules' which serve different kinds of knowledge and learning.

3   The language children are exposed to does not contain examples (or, in any case, not very many examples) of all the linguistic rules and patterns which they eventually know.

4   Animals—even primates receiving intensive training from humans—cannot learn to manipulate a symbol system as complicated as the natural language of a three- or four-year-old human child.

5   Children seem to accomplish the complex task of language acquisition without having someone consistently point out to them *which* of the sentences they hear and produce are 'correct' and which are 'ungrammatical'.

One example of the kind of complex language systems which children seem to learn without special guidance is the system of reflexive pronouns. This system of pronouns has been studied by a number of linguists working from a Chomskyan perspective.

Consider the following sentences which we have taken from a book by Lydia White (1989). These English sentences contain the reflexive pronoun 'himself'. Both the pronoun and the noun it refers to (the antecedent) are printed in *italics*. An asterisk at the beginning of a sentence indicates that the sentence is ungrammatical.

What do children have to discover about the relationship between the reflexive pronoun and its antecedent? Could they learn what they need to know by imitation of sentences they hear?

> a. *John* saw *himself.*
> b. **Himself* saw *John.*

In (a) and (b), it looks as if the reflexive pronoun must follow the noun it refers to. But (c) disproves this:

> c. Looking after *himself* bores *John.*

If we consider sentences such as:

> d. John said that *Fred* liked *himself.*
> e. **John* said that Fred liked *himself.*
> f. John told *Bill* to wash *himself.*
> g. **John* told Bill to wash *himself.*

we might conclude that the closest noun phrase is usually the antecedent. However, (h) shows that this rule won't work either:

> h. *John* promised Bill to wash *himself.*

And it's even more complicated than that. Usually the reflexive must be in the same clause as the antecedent as in (a) and (d), but not always, as in (h). Furthermore, the reflexive can be in the subject position in (i) but not in (j).

> i. *John* believes *himself* to be intelligent (non-finite clause).
> j. **John* believes that *himself* is intelligent (finite clause).

In some cases, more than one antecedent is possible, as in (k) where the reflexive could refer to either John or Bill:

> k. *John* showed *Bill* a picture of *himself.*

By now, you are probably quite convinced of the complexity of the rules pertaining to interpreting reflexive pronouns in English. The innatists argue that children could not discover the rules about reflexive pronouns by trial and error, even if parents did systematically correct children's errors. In fact, they simply do not make enough mistakes for this explanation to be plausible. The innatists conclude that a child's acquisition of these grammatical rules is guided by principles of an innate Universal Grammar which could apply to all languages. Children come to 'know' certain things about the specific language being learned through exposure to a limited number of examples. Different languages have different rules about, for example, reflexives, and children seem able to learn, on hearing *some* sentences, which *other* ones are possible and which are *not* in the language they are learning.

The biological basis for the innatist position

Chomsky's ideas are compatible with those of the biologist Eric Lenneberg, who also compares learning to talk with learning to walk: children who for medical reasons cannot move about when they are infants may soon stand and walk if their problems are corrected at the age of a year or so. Similarly, children who can hear but who cannot speak can nevertheless learn language, understanding even complex sentences.

The Critical Period Hypothesis

Lenneberg observed that this ability to develop normal behaviours and knowledge in a variety of environments does not continue indefinitely and that children who have never learned language (because of deafness or extreme isolation) cannot do so if these deprivations go on for too long. He argued that the language acquisition device, like other biological functions, works successfully only when it is stimulated at the right time—a time called the 'critical period'. This notion that there is a specific and limited time period for language acquisition is referred to as the Critical Period Hypothesis (CPH). Read the following case studies and think about whether they support the CPH.

Natural experiments: Victor and Genie

It is understandably difficult to find evidence for the Critical Period Hypothesis, since all normal children are exposed to language at an early age and consequently acquire language. However, history has documented a few 'natural experiments' where children have been deprived of contact with language. One of the most famous cases is that of a child called Victor. François Truffaut created a film, *L'Enfant sauvage* (*The Untamed Child*), about him and about the efforts to teach him to speak.

In 1799, a boy of about 12 years old was found wandering naked in the woods of Aveyron in France. Upon capture, he was found to be completely wild, apparently having had no contact with humankind. A young doctor, Jean-Marc-Gaspard Itard, devoted five years to the task of socializing Victor and trying to teach him language.

Although Itard succeeded to some extent in developing Victor's sociability, memory, judgement, and all the functions of his senses, Victor remained unreceptive to all sounds other than those which had meaning for him in the forest, such as the cracking of a nut, animal sounds, or the sound of rain. He only succeeded in speaking two words, his favourite food 'lait' (milk) and his governess's frequent exclamation 'O Dieu!' (Oh, God!). Moreover, his use of 'lait' was only uttered as an excited exclamation at the sight of a glass of milk. He never uttered the word to request milk, even though it was the one thing he could name, and something of which he was very fond. Even when Itard took Victor's milk away in hopes of making him ask for it, Victor never used the word to communicate his need. Finally, Itard gave up.

Another famous case of a child who did not learn language normally in her early years is that of Genie. Genie was discovered in California in 1970, a 13-year-old girl who had been isolated, deprived, neglected, and abused. Because of the irrational demands of a disturbed father and the submission and fear of an abused mother, Genie had spent more than eleven years tied to a chair or a crib in a small, darkened room. Her father had forbidden his wife and son to speak to her and had himself only growled and barked at her. She was beaten every time she vocalized or made any kind of noise, and she had long since resorted to complete silence. Genie was unsocialized, primitive, and undeveloped physically, emotionally, and intellectually. Needless to say, she had no language.

After she was discovered, Genie was cared for and educated in the most natural surroundings possible, and to the fullest extent possible, with the participation of many teachers and therapists. After a brief period in a rehabilitation centre, Genie lived in a foster home and attended special schools. Although far from being 'normal', Genie made remarkable progress in becoming socialized and cognitively aware. She developed deep personal relationships and strong individual tastes and traits. But despite the supportive environment for language acquisition, Genie's language development has not paralleled natural first language development. After five years of exposure to language, a period during which a normal child would have acquired an elaborated language system, Genie's language contained many of the features of abnormal language development. These include a larger than normal gap between comprehension and production, inconsistency in the use of grammatical forms, a slow *rate of development*, overuse of formulaic and routine speech, and the absence of some specific syntactic forms and mechanisms always present in normal grammatical development (Curtiss 1977). For discussion of further developments in Genie's life, see Rymer (1993).

Genie's language shares features of language development exhibited by adults with brain damage who have had to relearn language in adulthood, by children in the earliest stage of language acquisition, and by chimps attempting to learn language. It is the most carefully documented and tested case of a child brought up in isolation, allowing linguists to study the hypotheses regarding the critical period.

Although these cases appear to support the CPH, it is difficult to argue that the hypothesis is confirmed on the basis of evidence from such unusual children and the unknown circumstances of their early lives. We cannot know what other factors besides biological maturity (for example, social isolation or physical abuse) might have contributed to their inability to learn language. For now, the best evidence for the CPH is that virtually every child learns language on a schedule which is very similar in spite of quite different circumstances of life.

Both Victor and Genie were deprived of a normal home environment, which may account for their abnormal language development. There are other individuals, however, who come from loving homes, yet do not receive exposure to language at the usual time. This is the case of many profoundly deaf children who have hearing parents.

Natural experiments: Deaf signers

Elissa Newport and her colleagues have studied deaf users of American Sign Language (ASL) who acquired it as their first language at different ages. Such a population exists because only 5–10 per cent of the profoundly deaf are born to deaf parents, and only these children would be likely to be exposed to ASL from birth. The remainder of the profoundly deaf population begin learning ASL at different ages, often when they start attending a residential school where sign language is used for day-to-day communication.

In one study, there were three distinct groups of ASL users: Native signers who were exposed to sign language from birth, Early learners whose first exposure to ASL began at ages four to six at school, and Late learners who first came into contact with ASL after the age of 12 (Newport 1990).

Just like oral languages, ASL makes use of grammatical markers (like *-ed* and *-ing* in English); the only difference is that these markers are indicated through specific hand or body movements. The researchers were interested in whether there was any difference between Native signers, Early learners, and Late learners in the ability to produce and comprehend grammatical markers.

Results of the research showed a clear pattern. On word order, there was no difference between the groups. But on tests focusing on grammatical markers, the Native group outperformed the Early learner group who outperformed the Late learner group. The Native signers were highly consistent in their use of the grammatical forms. Although the other two groups used many of the same forms as the Native group, they also used forms which are considered ungrammatical by the Native signers. For example, they would omit certain grammatical forms, or use them in some obligatory contexts but not in others. The researchers conclude that their study supports the hypothesis that there is a critical period for first language acquisition.

We will return to a discussion of the CPH in Chapter 3 when we look at the age issue in second language acquisition.

Summary

The innatist position has been very persuasive in pointing out how complex the knowledge of adult speakers is and how difficult it is to account for the acquisition of this complex knowledge. Some researchers, however, have argued that the innatists have placed too much emphasis on the 'final state', that is, the competence of adult native speakers, and not enough on the developmental aspects of language acquisition.

A recent view of language acquisition which is attracting much attention is *connectionism*. Connectionists differ sharply from the Chomskyan innatists because they hypothesize that language acquisition does not require a separate 'module of the mind' but can be explained in terms of learning in general. Furthermore, connectionists argue that what children need to know is essentially available in the language they are exposed to. They use computer simulations to show that a computer program (relatively uncomplicated when compared to the human brain!) can 'learn' certain things if it is exposed to them often enough. The program can even generalize beyond what it has actually been exposed to and make the same kinds of creative 'mistakes' that children make. Linguists working in the UG framework challenge connectionists to show that their theory can account for complex syntax as well as for the learning of words and grammatical morphemes, and the debate between the proponents of these two positions promises to be lively for many years to come.

The interactionist position: A little help from my friends

A third theoretical view of first language acquisition focuses on the role of the linguistic environment in interaction with the child's innate capacities in determining language development.

The *interactionists'* position is that language develops as a result of the complex interplay between the uniquely human characteristics of the child and the environment in which the child develops. Interactionists attribute considerably more importance to the environment than the innatists do. For example, unlike the innatists, most interactionists claim that language which is modified to suit the capability of the learner is a crucial element in the language acquisition process. They emphasize the importance of *child-directed speech*—the language which is not only addressed to children but adjusted in ways that make it easier for them to understand. In addition, interactionists are inclined to see language acquisition as similar to and influenced by the acquisition of other kinds of skill and knowledge, rather than as something which is largely independent of the child's experience and cognitive development. However, interactionists represent a wide range of theories about the relative contributions of innate structures of the human mind and the environment which provides the samples of the language to be learned.

Among interactionist positions we could include those which were articulated much earlier in this century by the Swiss psychologist/epistomologist, Jean Piaget (see Ginsburg and Opper 1969). Piaget observed infants and children in their play and in their interaction with adults. He was able to trace the development of their cognitive understanding of such things as object permanence (knowing that things which are hidden from sight are still there), the stability of quantities regardless of changes in their appearance (knowing that ten pennies spread out to form a long line are not more numerous than ten pennies in a tightly squeezed line), and logical inferencing (figuring out which properties of a set of rods—size, weight, material, etc.—cause some rods to sink and others to float on water). It is easy to see from this how children's cognitive development would partly determine how they use language. For example, the use of certain terms such as 'bigger' or 'more' depend on the children's understanding of the concepts they represent. The developing cognitive understanding is built on the interaction between the child and the things which can be observed, touched, and manipulated.

Unlike the innatists, Piaget did not see language as based on a separate module of the mind. For him, language was one of a number of symbol systems which are developed in childhood. Language can be used to represent knowledge that children have acquired through physical interaction with the environment.

A strongly interactionist view was the sociocultural theory of human mental processing held by the psychologist Lev Vygotsky who worked in the Soviet Union in the 1920s and 1930s (Vygotsky 1978). He concluded that language develops entirely from social interaction. He argued that in a supportive interactive environment, the child is able to advance to a higher level of knowledge and performance than he or she would be capable of independently. Vygotsky referred to what the child could do in interaction with another, but not alone, as the child's *zone of proximal development.* He observed the importance of conversations which children have with adults and with other children and saw in these conversations the origins of both language and thought. Vygotsky's view differs from Piaget's. Piaget hypothesized that language developed as a symbol system to express knowledge acquired through interaction with the physical world. For Vygotsky, thought was essentially internalized speech, and speech emerged in social interaction.

Child-directed speech

Many researchers have studied child-directed speech, the language which adults use with children. We are all familiar with the way adults frequently modify the way they speak when addressing little children. In English, child-directed speech involves a slower rate of delivery, higher pitch, more varied intonation, shorter, simpler sentence patterns, frequent repetition, and paraphrase. Furthermore, topics of conversation may be limited to the child's immediate environment, the 'here and now', or to experiences which the adult knows the child has had. Adults often repeat the content of a child's utterance, but they expand it into a grammatically correct sentence. If you examine the transcripts presented earlier in this chapter, you will see examples of some of these features. For example, when Peter says, 'Dump truck! Dump truck! Fall! Fall!', Lois responds, 'Yes, the dump truck fell down.'

Researchers working among parents and children from a variety of cultural groups have found that the child-directed speech which was described on the basis of studies of families in middle-class American homes is not universal. In some societies, adults do not engage in conversation or verbal play with very young children. And yet these children achieve full competence in the community language. Thus, it is difficult to judge the importance of these modifications which some adults make in speech addressed to children. Children whose parents do not consistently provide such *modified interaction* will still learn language; however, they may have access to modified language when they are in the company of older siblings or other children. To the theorist, this suggests that more important than simplification is the conversational give-and-take in which the more proficient speaker intuitively responds to the clues the child provides as to the level of language he or she is capable of processing. The importance of such interaction becomes abundantly clear in the atypical cases where it is missing. Such is the case of Jim.

Case study: Jim

Jim, the hearing child of deaf parents, had little contact with hearing/ speaking adults up to the age of three years and nine months (3,9). His only contact with oral language was through television, which he watched frequently. The family was unusual in that the parents did not use sign language with Jim. Thus, although in other respects he was well cared for, Jim did not begin his linguistic development in a normal environment in which a parent communicated with him in either oral or sign language. Language tests administered indicated that he was very much below age level in all aspects of language. Although he attempted to express ideas appropriate to his age, he used unusual, ungrammatical word order.

When Jim began conversational sessions with an adult, his expressive abilities began to improve. By the age of 4,2 most of the unusual speech patterns had disappeared, replaced by structures more typical of Jim's age. It is interesting to note that Jim's younger brother Glenn did not display the same type of lag and performed normally on language tests when he was the age at which Jim was first tested. Glenn's linguistic environment was different in that he had his older brother as a conversational partner (Sachs, Bard, and Johnson 1981).

Jim showed very rapid acquisition of the structures of English once he began to interact with an adult on a one-to-one basis. The fact that he had failed to acquire language normally prior to this experience suggests that the problem lay in the environment, not the child. That is, it seems that exposure to impersonal sources of language such as television or radio alone is insufficient for the child to learn the structure of a particular language.

One-to-one interaction gives the child access to language which is adjusted to his or her level of comprehension. When a child does not understand, the adult may repeat or paraphrase. The response of the adult may also allow children to find out when their own utterances are understood. Television, for obvious reasons, does not provide such interaction. Even in children's programs, where simpler language is used and topics are relevant to younger viewers, there is no immediate adjustment made for the needs of an individual child.

Summary

We have presented three different broad theoretical approaches to explaining first language acquisition, each of which can be corroborated by evidence. As we have seen in the transcripts from Peter and Cindy (pages 10–12), children *do* imitate and practise, and practice can explain how some aspects of the language such as word meanings and some language routines are learned. We saw in the example of reflexive pronouns, however, that imitation and practice alone cannot account for the complexity of the knowledge that all children eventually attain. The acquisition of such complex language seems to depend on children's possession of some knowledge which permits them to process the language they hear and to go well beyond this and even beyond simple generalizations. The discussion of the interactionist position (especially the case of Jim) showed that children who are exposed to language in the absence of one-to-one interaction do not develop language normally.

One way to reconcile the behaviourist, innatist, and interactionist theories is to see that each may help to explain a different aspect of children's language development. Behaviourist and connectionist explanations may explain the acquisition of vocabulary and grammatical morphemes. Innatist explanations seem most plausible in explaining the acquisition of complex grammar. Interactionist explanations may be useful for understanding how children relate form and meaning in language, how they interact in conversations, and how they learn to use language appropriately.

In Chapter 2 we will begin to look at the acquisition of second languages by children and older learners. We will see that many of the issues raised in this chapter will be relevant to our discussion of second language acquisition.

Sources and suggestions for further reading

General accounts of first language acquisition

Baron, N. 1992. *Growing Up with Language.* Reading, Mass.: Addison-Wesley.

Berko Gleason, J. 1989. *The Development of Language.* Columbus, Ohio: Merrill.

Bloom, L. and **M. Lahey.** 1978. *Language Development and Language Disorders.* New York: John Wiley.

de Villiers, J. G. and **P. A. de Villiers.** 1978. *Language Acquisition.* Cambridge, Mass.: Harvard University Press.

Ingram, D. 1989. *First Language Acquisition: Method, Description and Explanation.* Cambridge: Cambridge University Press.

Perception of speech sounds in infancy

Eimas, P. D., E. Siquelard, P. Jusczyk, and **P. J. Vigorito.** 1979. 'Speech perception in infants.' *Science* 171/3968: 303–6.

Developmental sequences

Brown, R. 1973. *A First Language: The Early Stages*. Cambridge, Mass.: Harvard University Press.

de Villiers, J. G. and **P. A. de Villiers.** 1973. 'A cross-sectional study of the acquisition of grammatical morphemes.' *Journal of Psycholinguistic Research* 2/3: 267–78.

Imitation in first language acquisition

Bloom, L., L. Hood, and **P. M. Lightbown.** 1974. 'Imitation in child language: if, when, and why'. *Cognitive Psychology* 6/3: 380–420. Reprinted in L. Bloom and M. Lahey. 1978. *Readings in Language Development*. New York: John Wiley.

Early childhood bilingualism

Arenberg, L. 1987. *Raising Children Bilingually: The Pre-school Years*. Clevedon, UK: Multilingual Matters.

Baker, C. 1995. *A Parents' and Teachers' Guide to Bilingualism*. Clevedon, UK: Multilingual Matters.

Döpke, S. 1992. *One Parent One Language: An Interactional Approach*. Amsterdam: John Benjamins.

Genesee, F. (ed.). 1995. *Educating Second Language Children: The Whole Child, the Whole Curriculum, the Whole Community*. Cambridge: Cambridge University Press.

Saunders, G. 1988. *Bilingual Children: From Birth to Teens*. Clevedon, UK: Multilingual Matters.

Chomsky's innatist ideas

Chomsky, N. 1959. Review of *Verbal Behavior* by B. F. Skinner. *Language* 35/1: 26–58.

Chomsky, N. 1981. *Lectures on Government and Binding*. Dordrecht: Foris. Chapter 1.

Cook, V. 1988. *Chomsky's Universal Grammar*. London: Basil Blackwell.

Lenneberg, E. 1967. *The Biological Foundations of Language*. New York, John Wiley.

Pinker, S. 1994. *The Language Instinct*. New York: William Morrow.

White L. 1989. *Universal Grammar and Second Language Acquisition*. Amsterdam/Philadelphia, Pa.: John Benjamins.

Connectionism

Elman, J. L., E. A. Bates, M. H. Johnson, A. Karmiloff-Smith, D. Parisi, and **K. Plunkett.** 1996. *Rethinking Innateness: A Connectionist Perspective on Development.* Cambridge, Mass.: MIT Press.

Piaget

Ginsburg, H. and **S. Opper.** 1969. *Piaget's Theory of Intellectual Development: An Introduction.* Englewood Cliffs, N.J.: Prentice-Hall.

Vygotsky

Vygotsky, L. S. 1978. *Mind and Society.* Cambridge, Mass.: Harvard University Press.

Wertsch, J. V. 1985. *Vygotsky and the Social Formation of Mind.* Cambridge, Mass.: Harvard University Press.

Genie

Curtiss, S. 1977. *Genie: A Psycholinguistic Study of a Modern-day 'Wild Child.'* New York: Academic Press.

Rymer, R. 1993. *Genie: A Scientific Tragedy.* New York: HarperCollins.

L'enfant sauvage

Itard, J.-M.-G. 1962. *The Wild Boy of Aveyron (L'Enfant sauvage).* New York: Meredith.

Child-directed speech

Snow, C. E., and **C. A. Ferguson.** (eds.). 1977. *Talking to Children: Language Input and Acquisition.* Cambridge: Cambridge University Press.

Differences in parent–child interaction in different sociocultural groups

Crago, M. 1992. 'Communicative interaction and second language acquisition: An Inuit example.' *TESOL Quarterly* 26/3: 487–505.

Heath, S. B. 1983. *Ways with Words.* Cambridge: Cambridge University Press.

Schieffelin, B. 1990. *The Give and Take of Everyday Life: Language Socialization of Kaluli Children.* Cambridge: Cambridge University Press.

Schieffelin, B. and **E. Ochs.** (eds.). 1986. *Language Socialization across Cultures.* Cambridge: Cambridge University Press.

Learning American Sign Language at different ages

Newport, E. 1990. 'Maturational constraints on language learning.' *Cognitive Science* 14/1: 11–28.

Case study of Jim

Sachs, J., B. Bard, and **M. Johnson.** 1981. 'Language learning with restricted input: case studies of two hearing children of deaf parents.' *Applied Psycholinguistics* 2/1: 33–54.

2 THEORETICAL APPROACHES TO EXPLAINING SECOND LANGUAGE LEARNING

In this chapter we look at some of the theories that have been proposed to account for *second language acquisition* (SLA). In many ways, theories which have been developed for SLA are closely related to those discussed for first language acquisition in Chapter 1. That is, some theories give primary importance to learners' innate characteristics; some emphasize the essential role of the environment in shaping language learning; still others seek to integrate learner characteristics and environmental factors in an explanation for how second language acquisition takes place.

It is clear that a child or adult learning a second language is different from a child acquiring a first language in terms of both personal characteristics and conditions for learning. Questions to consider include:

1 Does the learner already know a language?

2 Is the learner cognitively mature, that is, is he or she able to engage in problem solving, deduction, and complex memory tasks?

3 How well developed is the learner's metalinguistic awareness? That is, can the learner treat language as an object—for example, define a word, say what sounds make up that word, or state a rule such as 'add an -s to form the plural'?

4 How extensive is the learner's general knowledge of the world? This kind of knowledge makes it easier to understand language because one can sometimes make good guesses about what the interlocutor is probably saying even when the language carrying the message is new.

5 Is the learner nervous about making mistakes and sounding 'silly' when speaking the language?

6 Does the learning environment allow the learner to be silent in the early stages of learning, or is he or she expected to speak from the beginning?

7 Is there plenty of time available for language learning to take place, plenty of contact with proficient speakers of the language?

8 Does the learner receive *corrective feedback* when he or she makes errors in grammar or pronunciation, or does the listener overlook these errors and pay attention to the message?

9 Does the learner receive corrective feedback when he or she uses the wrong word, or does the listener usually try to guess the intended meaning?

10 Is the learner exposed to language which is modified, in terms of speed of delivery, complexity of grammatical structure, and vocabulary, so that it matches the learner's ability to comprehend and interact?

Activity

Learner profiles

Table 2.1 helps to illustrate possible answers to these questions with respect to the profiles of four language learners:

– a child learning its first language (L1)
– a child learning a second language (L2) informally
– an adolescent learning a second language in a *formal language learning setting*
– an adult learning a second language informally (in the workplace or among friends).

Fill in the chart, giving your opinion about the presence or absence of the characteristics or conditions referred to in the questions above. Use the following notation:
+ = a characteristic which is usually present
– = a characteristic which is usually absent
? = where the characteristic or condition is sometimes present, sometimes absent, or where you are not sure.

The discussion below summarizes our views about the profiles of these four language learners in terms of their characteristics and the conditions in which their learning takes place.

Learner characteristics

All second language learners, regardless of age, have by definition already acquired at least one language. This prior knowledge may be an advantage in the sense that the learner has an idea of how languages work. On the other hand, as we shall see, knowledge of other languages can also lead learners to make incorrect guesses about how the second language works and this may cause errors which a first language learner would not make.

Young language learners begin the task of language learning without the benefit of some of the skills and knowledge which adolescent and adult learners have. The first language learner does not have the same *cognitive*

	LI	L2		
Learner characteristics	*Child*	*Child (informal)*	*Adolescent (formal)*	*Adult (informal)*
1 knowledge of another language				
2 cognitive maturity				
3 metalinguistic awareness				
4 knowledge of the world				
5 nervousness about speaking				
Learning conditions				
6 freedom to be silent				
7 ample time				
8 corrective feedback: grammar and pronunciation				
9 corrective feedback: word choice				
10 modified input				

maturity, metalinguistic awareness, or world knowledge as older second language learners. Although young second language learners have begun to develop cognitive maturity and metalinguistic awareness, they will still have far to go in these areas, as well as in the area of world knowledge, before they reach the levels already attained by adults and adolescents.

Most child learners do not feel nervous about attempting to use the language—even when their proficiency is quite limited, but adults and adolescents often find it very stressful when they are unable to express themselves clearly and correctly. Nevertheless, even very young (pre-school) children differ in their nervousness when faced with speaking a language they do not know well. Some children happily chatter away in their new language; others prefer to listen and participate silently in social interaction with their peers. Fortunately for these children, the learning environment rarely puts pressure on them to speak when they are not ready.

Learning conditions
Younger learners, in an informal second language learning environment, are usually allowed to be silent until they are ready to speak. Older learners are often forced to speak—to meet the requirements of a classroom or to carry out everyday tasks such as shopping, medical visits, or job interviews. Young children in informal settings are usually exposed to the second language for

many hours every day. Older learners, especially students in language classrooms, are more likely to receive only limited exposure to the second language.

One condition which appears to be common to learners of all ages—though perhaps not in equal quantities—is access to *modified input*. This adjusted speech style, which is called child-directed speech for first languages, is sometimes called *foreigner talk* or *teacher talk* for second languages. Many people who interact regularly with language learners seem to have an intuitive sense of what adjustments are needed to help learners understand. Of course, some people are better at this than others. We have all witnessed those painful conversations in which insensitive people seem to think that they can make learners understand better if they simply talk louder! Some Canadian friends recently told us of an experience they had in China. They were visiting some historic temples and wanted to get more information about them than they could glean from their guidebook. They asked their guide some questions about the monuments. Unfortunately, their limited Chinese and his non-existent English made it difficult for them to exchange information. The guide kept speaking louder and louder, but our friends understood very little. Finally, in frustration, the guide concluded that it would help if these hopeless foreigners could *see* the information—so he took a stick and began writing in the sand—in Chinese characters!

As we saw in Chapter 1, error correction in first language acquisition tends to be limited to corrections of meaning—including errors in vocabulary choice. In informal second language acquisition, errors which do not interfere with meaning are usually overlooked. Most people would feel they were being impolite if they interrupted and corrected someone who was trying to have a conversation with them! Nevertheless, they may react to an error if they cannot understand what the speaker is trying to say. Thus, errors of grammar and pronunciation are rarely remarked on, but the wrong word choice may receive comment from a puzzled interlocutor. The only place where feedback on error is typically present with high frequency is the language classroom. As we shall see, however, it is not present in all classrooms.

Summary

A general theory of SLA needs to account for language acquisition by learners with a variety of characteristics, learning in a variety of contexts. The emphasis in this chapter is on the theories which have been proposed to explain the learning mechanisms which are common to all second language learners. In Chapter 3, we will look at proposals for how differences among learners may lead to differences in their learning success.

Behaviourism

In this section, we will discuss the impact of behaviourism on our understanding of second language learning. Later in this chapter, we will discuss some more recent theories based on cognitive psychology.

As we saw in Chapter 1, behaviourists account for learning in terms of imitation, practice, reinforcement (or feedback on success), and habit formation. According to the behaviourists, all learning, whether verbal or non-verbal, takes place through the same underlying processes. Learners receive linguistic input from speakers in their environment and they form 'associations' between words and objects or events. These associations become stronger as experiences are repeated. Learners receive encouragement for their correct imitations, and corrective feedback on their errors. Because language development is viewed as the formation of habits, it is assumed that a person learning a second language starts off with the habits formed in the first language and that these habits interfere with the new ones needed for the second language (Lado 1964).

Behaviourism was often linked to the *Contrastive Analysis Hypothesis* (CAH) which was developed by structural linguists in Europe and North America. The CAH predicts that where there are similarities between the first language and the *target language*, the learner will acquire target-language structures with ease; where there are differences, the learner will have difficulty.

There is little doubt that a learner's first language influences the acquisition of a second language. However, researchers have found that not all errors predicted by the CAH are actually made. Furthermore, many of the errors which learners do make are not predictable on the basis of the CAH. For example, adult beginners use simple structures in the target language just as children do: 'No understand,' or 'Yesterday I meet my teacher.' Such sentences look more like a child's first language sentences than like translations from another language. Indeed, many of the sentences produced by second language learners in the early stages of development would be quite ungrammatical in their first language. What is more, some characteristics of these simple structures are very similar across learners from a variety of backgrounds, even if the structures of their respective first languages are different from each other and different from the target language.

In Chapter 4, we will see that learners are reluctant to transfer certain features of their first language to the second language, even when the translation equivalent would be correct. All this suggests that the influence of the learner's first language may not simply be a matter of the transfer of habits, but a more subtle and complex process of identifying points of similarity, weighing the evidence in support of some particular feature, and even reflecting (though not necessarily consciously) about whether a certain feature seems to 'belong' in the structure of the target language.

For second language acquisition, as for first language acquisition, the behaviourist account has proven to be at best an incomplete explanation for language learning. Psychologists have proposed new, more complex theories of learning. Some of these are discussed later in this chapter.

Innatism

Universal Grammar

As we saw in Chapter 1, Chomsky's theory of language acquisition is based on the hypothesis that innate knowledge of the principles of Universal Grammar (UG) permits all children to acquire the language of their environment, during a critical period in their development. Chomsky has not made specific claims about the implications of his theory for *second* language learning. Nevertheless, some linguists working within this theory have argued that Universal Grammar offers the best perspective from which to understand second language acquisition (SLA). Others argue that, although it is a good framework for understanding first language acquisition, UG is no longer available to guide the acquisition of a second language in learners who have passed the critical period for language acquisition. In their view, this means that second language acquisition has to be explained by some other theory, perhaps one of the more recent psychological theories described below.

Even those who believe that UG has an important explanatory role in SLA do not all agree on how UG works in second language development. Some argue that, even if second language learners begin learning the second language after the end of the critical period and even if many fail to achieve complete mastery of the target language, there is still a logical problem of (second) language acquisition: learners eventually know more about the language than they could reasonably have learned if they had to depend entirely on the input they are exposed to. They infer from this that UG must be available to second language learners as well as to first language learners. Some of the theorists who hold this view claim that the nature and availability of UG in SLA is no different from that which is hypothesized to guide first language learners. Others argue that UG may be present and available to second language learners, but that its exact nature has been altered by the acquisition of other languages.

Researchers working within the UG framework also differ in their hypotheses about how formal instruction or error correction will affect the learner's knowledge of the second language. Some argue that, like young children, adult second language learners neither need nor benefit from error correction and metalinguistic information. They conclude that these things change only the superficial appearance of language performance and do not really affect the underlying systematic knowledge of the new language (Schwartz 1993 and see the discussion of Krashen's theory, on pages 38–40). Other UG linguists, especially those who think that UG has been affected by the prior acquisition of the first language, suggest that second language learners may need to be given some explicit information about what is *not* grammatical in the second language. Otherwise, they may assume that some structures of the first language have equivalents in the second language when, in fact, they do not. (See further discussion and an example in Chapter 4.)

Researchers who study SLA from the UG perspective are usually interested in the language *competence* (knowledge) of advanced learners rather than in the simple language of early stage learners. They argue that, while a variety of different theories might be sufficient to explain some early language *performance* (use), a theory such as UG is necessary to explain learners' knowledge of complex syntax. They are interested in whether the competence which underlies the language performance of second language learners resembles the competence which underlies the language performance of native speakers. Thus their investigations often involve comparing the *judgements of grammaticality* made by the two groups, rather than observations of actual speaking. In doing this, they hope to gain insight into what learners actually know about the language, using a task which avoids at least some of the many things which affect the way we ordinarily *use* language.

Krashen's 'monitor model'

An innatist theory of second language acquisition which has had a very great influence on second language teaching practice is the one proposed by Stephen Krashen (1982). Five 'hypotheses' constitute what Krashen originally called the 'monitor model'. He claims that research findings from a number of different domains are consistent with these hypotheses: (1) the acquisition–learning hypothesis; (2) the monitor hypothesis; (3) the natural order hypothesis; (4) the input hypothesis; and (5) the affective filter hypothesis.

1 The acquisition–learning hypothesis

According to Krashen, there are two ways for adult second language learners to develop knowledge of a second language: 'acquisition' and 'learning'. In his view, we *acquire* as we are exposed to samples of the second language which we understand. This happens in much the same way that children pick up their first language—with no conscious attention to language form. We *learn*, on the other hand, via a conscious process of study and attention to form and rule learning.

For Krashen, acquisition is by far the more important process. He asserts that only acquired language is readily available for natural, fluent communication. Further, he asserts that learning cannot turn into acquisition. He cites as evidence for this that many speakers are quite fluent without ever having learned rules, while other speakers may 'know' rules but fail to apply them when they are focusing their attention on *what* they want to say more than on *how* they are saying it.

2 The monitor hypothesis

Krashen argues that the acquired system acts to initiate the speaker's utterances and is responsible for fluency and intuitive judgements about correctness. The learned system, on the other hand, acts only as an editor or 'monitor', making minor changes and polishing what the acquired system has produced. Moreover, Krashen has specified that learners use the monitor only when they are focused more on being 'correct' than on what they have to say, when they have sufficient time to search their memory for the relevant rules, and when they actually know those rules! Thus, writing may be more conducive than speaking to monitor use, because it usually allows more time for attention to form. He maintains that since knowing the rules only helps the speaker supplement what has been acquired, the focus of language teaching should be on creating conditions for 'acquisition' rather than 'learning'.

It is very difficult to show evidence of 'monitor' use. In any given utterance, it is impossible to determine what has been produced by the acquired system and what is the result of monitor use. Krashen's claim that language which is produced quickly and apparently spontaneously must have been acquired rather than learned leaves us with a somewhat circular definition.

3 The natural order hypothesis

Krashen based this hypothesis on the observation that, like first language learners, second language learners seem to acquire the features of the target language in predictable sequences. Contrary to intuition, the rules which are easiest to state (and thus to 'learn') are not necessarily the first to be acquired. For example, the rule for adding an -*s* to third person singular verbs in the present tense is easy to state, but even some advanced second language speakers fail to apply it in rapid conversation. Further, Krashen observes that the *natural order* is independent of the order in which rules have been learned in language classes. Most of Krashen's original evidence for this hypothesis came from the 'morpheme studies', in which learners' speech was examined for the accuracy of certain *grammatical morphemes*. While there have been many criticisms of the morpheme studies, subsequent research has confirmed that learners pass through sequences or stages in development. In Chapter 4, we will look at some of these sequences in second language acquisition.

4 The input hypothesis

Krashen asserts that one acquires language in only one way—by exposure to *comprehensible input*. If the input contains forms and structures just beyond the learner's current level of competence in the language (what Krashen calls 'i + 1'), then both comprehension and acquisition will occur.

Krashen cites many varied lines of evidence for this hypothesis, most of which appeal to intuition, but which have not been substantiated by empirical studies. In recent years, he has emphasized the value of undirected pleasure reading as a source of comprehensible input. While he acknowledges that some people who are exposed to extensive comprehensible input do not achieve high levels of proficiency in the second language, he retains his conviction that input is the source of acquisition. He points to the affective filter hypothesis to explain lack of success when comprehensible input is available.

5 The affective filter hypothesis

The 'affective filter' is an imaginary barrier which prevents learners from acquiring language from the available input. 'Affect' refers to such things as motives, needs, attitudes, and emotional states. A learner who is tense, angry, anxious, or bored may 'filter out' input, making it unavailable for acquisition. Thus, depending on the learner's state of mind or disposition, the filter limits what is noticed and what is acquired. The filter will be 'up' (blocking input) when the learner is stressed, self-conscious, or unmotivated. It will be 'down' when the learner is relaxed and motivated.

What makes this hypothesis attractive to practitioners is that it appears to have immediate implications for classroom practice. Teachers can understand why some learners, given the same opportunity to learn, may be successful while others are not. It also appeals intuitively to those who have tried unsuccessfully to learn a language in conditions where they felt stressed or uncomfortable. One problem with the hypothesis, however, is that it is difficult to be sure that affective factors *cause* the differences in language acquisition. It seems likely that success in acquisition may in itself contribute to more positive motivation or, in Krashen's terms, to a 'lowered affective filter'. In Chapter 3, we will discuss further the relationship between attitudes/motivation and success in second language learning.

Krashen's writing has been very influential in supporting *communicative language teaching* (CLT), particularly in North America. On the other hand, the theory has also been seriously criticized for failing to propose hypotheses which can be tested by empirical research. Most teachers and researchers see much which is intuitively appealing in his views. There is little doubt that communicative language teaching, with its primary focus on using language for meaningful interaction and for accomplishing tasks, rather than on learning rules, has won support from many teachers and learners. Nevertheless, it will be seen in Chapter 6 that some classroom-centred research shows that attention to language form may be more important than Krashen acknowledges. We will also see that instruction which focuses on language form can be incorporated within communicative language teaching.

Recent psychological theories

Information processing

Cognitive psychologists working in an *information processing* model of human learning and performance tend to see second language acquisition as the building up of knowledge systems that can eventually be called on automatically for speaking and understanding. At first, learners have to pay attention to any aspect of the language which they are trying to understand or produce. It is assumed that there is a limit to the amount of information a human can pay attention to at one time. Thus, for example, a learner at the earliest stages of second language learning will probably pay attention to the main words in a message and not be able to also notice the grammatical morphemes which are attached to some of those words. Gradually, through experience and practice, learners become able to use certain parts of their knowledge so quickly and automatically that they are not even aware that they are doing it. This frees them to focus on other aspects of the language which, in turn, gradually become automatic (McLaughlin 1987). The performance which will eventually become automatic may originate from intentional learning, for example in formal study, but this is not always the case. Anything which uses up our mental 'processing space', even if we are not aware of it or attending to it 'on purpose', is a possible source for information or skills which can eventually be available automatically, if there has been enough practice. Note that, in this context, 'practice' is not seen as something mechanical, but as something which involves effort on the part of the learner.

One theorist who has emphasized the role of 'noticing' in second language acquisition is Richard Schmidt. He argues that everything we come to know about the language was first 'noticed' consciously. This contrasts sharply with Krashen's views, of course. Schmidt, like the cognitive psychologists, does not assume that there is a difference between acquisition and learning (Schmidt 1990).

In addition to the development of automaticity through practice, some psychologists suggest that there are changes in skill and knowledge which are due to 'restructuring'. This notion is needed to account for the observation that sometimes things which we know and use automatically may not be explainable in terms of a gradual build-up of automaticity through practice. They seem rather to be based on the interaction of knowledge we already have, or on the acquisition of new knowledge which—without extensive practice— somehow fits into an existing system and causes it to be transformed or 'restructured'. This may lead to what appear to be sudden bursts of progress for the learner, but it can also sometimes lead to apparent backsliding when a systematic aspect of learner language incorporates too much or incorporates the wrong things. For example, when a learner finally masters the use of the regular *-ed* ending to show past tense, irregular verbs, which had previously been 'practised' correctly, may be affected. Thus, after months of saying 'I saw a film', the learner may say 'I seed' or even 'I sawed', overapplying the general rule.

Connectionism

As seen in the discussion of first language acquisition, connectionists, unlike innatists, see no need to hypothesize the existence of a neurological module which is designed for language acquisition alone. Like most cognitive psychologists, connectionists attribute greater importance to the role of the environment than to any innate knowledge in the learner, arguing that what is innate is simply the ability to learn, not any specifically linguistic structure.

Connectionists argue that learners gradually build up their knowledge of language through exposure to thousands of instances of the linguistic features they eventually learn. Thus, while innatists see the language input in the environment mainly as a 'trigger' to activate innate knowledge, connectionists see the input as the principal source of linguistic knowledge. After hearing language features in specific situational or linguistic contexts over and over again, learners develop stronger and stronger mental or neurological 'connections' between these elements. Eventually, the presence of one situational or linguistic element will activate the other(s) in the learner's mind. These connections may be very strong because the elements have occurred together very frequently or they may be relatively weaker because there have been fewer opportunities to experience them together. For example, learners might get the subject–verb agreement correct, not because they know a rule but because they have heard examples such as 'I say' and 'he says' so often that each subject pronoun activates the correct verb form.

As noted in Chapter 1, connectionist research has shown that a learning mechanism, simulated by a computer program, can not only 'learn' what it hears but can also generalize, even to the point of making overgeneralization errors. These studies have so far dealt almost exclusively with the acquisition of vocabulary and grammatical morphemes, that is, aspects of the language which even innatists will grant may be acquired largely through memorization and simple generalization. How this model of cumulative learning can lead to knowledge of complex syntactic structures is a question which is currently under investigation.

The interactionist position

Some interactionist theorists, while influenced by psychological learning theories, have developed their ideas mainly within SLA research itself. Evelyn

Hatch (1992), Teresa Pica (1994) and Michael Long (1983), among others, have argued that much second language acquisition takes place through conversational interaction. This is similar to the first language theory that gives great importance to child-directed speech. Michael Long's views are based on his observation of interactions between learners and native speakers. He agrees with Krashen that comprehensible input is necessary for language acquisition. However, he is more concerned with the question of *how* input is made comprehensible. He sees modified interaction as the necessary mechanism for this to take place (Long 1983). In his view, what learners need is not necessarily simplification of the linguistic forms but rather an opportunity to interact with other speakers, in ways which lead them to adapt what they are saying until the learner shows signs of understanding. According to Long, there are no cases of beginning-level learners acquiring a second language from native-speaker talk which has *not* been modified in some way. In fact, he says, research shows that native speakers consistently modify their speech in sustained conversation with non-native speakers.

Long infers that modified interaction must be necessary for language acquisition. This relationship has been summarized as follows:

1 Interactional modification makes input comprehensible;

2 Comprehensible input promotes acquisition.

Therefore,

3 Interactional modification promotes acquisition.

Modified interaction does not always involve linguistic simplification. It may also include elaboration, slower speech rate, gesture, or the provision of additional contextual cues. Some examples of these conversational modifications are:

1 Comprehension checks—efforts by the native speaker to ensure that the learner has understood (for example, 'The bus leaves at 6:30. Do you understand?').

2 Clarification requests—efforts by the learner to get the native speaker to clarify something which has not been understood (for example, 'Could you repeat please?'). These requests from the learner lead to further modifications by the native speaker.

3 Self-repetition or paraphrase—the native speaker repeats his or her sentence either partially or in its entirety (for example, 'She got lost on her way home from school. She was walking home from school. She got lost.').

Research has demonstrated that conversational adjustments can aid comprehension. There is evidence that modification which takes place during interaction leads to better understanding than linguistic simplification or modification which is planned in advance. While some recent research has shown that specific kinds of interaction behaviours aid learning in terms of immediate production, more research is needed on how access to modified interaction affects second language acquisition in the long term.

Another perspective on the role of interaction in second language acquisition is Vygotsky's sociocultural theory of human mental processing. As we saw in Chapter 1, Vygotsky's theory assumes that all cognitive development, including language development, arises as a result of social interactions between individuals. Extending Vygotskyan theory to second language acquisition, Jim Lantolf and others claim that second language learners advance to higher levels of linguistic knowledge when they collaborate and interact with speakers of the second language who are more knowledgeable than they are, for example, a teacher or a more advanced learner. Critical to Vygotsky's theory is the notion of the zone of proximal development, the level of performance which a learner is capable of when there is support from interaction with a more advanced interlocutor. This may be observed in a variety of speech strategies used by more advanced speakers to create supportive conditions for the second language learner to comprehend and produce language (for example, repetition, simplification, modelling). One example of this is the conversation below, reported by Richard Donato, who investigated how adult learners of French were able to co-construct language learning experiences in a classroom setting.

> **Speaker 1** ... and then I'll say ... *tu as souvenu notre anniversaire de mariage* ... or should I say *mon anniversaire?*
> **Speaker 2** *Tu as ...*
> **Speaker 3** *Tu as ...*
> **Speaker 1** *Tu as souvenu...* 'You remembered?'
> **Speaker 3** Yea, but isn't that reflexive? *Tu t'as ...*
> **Speaker 1** Ah, *tu t'as souvenu.*
> **Speaker 2** Oh, it's *tu es*
> **Speaker 1** *Tu es*
> **Speaker 3** *Tu es, tu es, tu ...*
> **Speaker 1** *T'es, tu t'es*
> **Speaker 3** *Tu t'es*
> **Speaker 1** *Tu t'es souvenu*

(Donato 1994: 44)

According to Vygotskyan theorists, the difference between this perspective and that of other researchers who also view interaction as important in second language acquisition is that sociocultural theorists assume that language acquisition actually takes place in the interactions of learner and interlocutor, whereas other interactionist models assume that input modification provides learners with the linguistic raw material which they will process internally and invisibly.

Summary

In the end, what all theories of language acquisition are meant to account for is the working of the human mind. All of the theories discussed in this chapter and in Chapter 1 use metaphors to represent this invisible reality. Both linguists and psychologists draw some of their evidence from neurological research. However, in light of the present state of technology as well as research ethics, most of the research must be based on other kinds of evidence.

Many claims from behaviourist theory were based on experiments with animals learning a variety of responses to laboratory stimuli. Their applicability to the natural learning of languages by humans was strongly challenged by psychologists and linguists alike, primarily because of the inadequacy of behaviourist models to account for the complexity involved in language learning.

Information processing and connectionist research often involves computer simulations or very controlled laboratory experiments where people learn a specific set of carefully chosen linguistic features, often in an invented language. Many linguists argue that this does not entitle connectionists to generalize to the complexities of normal human language learning.

In contrast, the innatists draw much of their evidence from studies of the complexities of the proficient speaker's language knowledge and performance and from analysis of their own intuitions about language. Critics of this view argue that it is not enough to know what the final state of knowledge is and that more attention should be paid to the developmental steps leading up to this level of mastery.

Interactionists emphasize the role of the modification of interaction in conversations. This helps us understand some of the ways in which learners can gain access to new knowledge about the language when they have support from an interlocutor. However, critics of the interactionist position argue that there is much which learners need to know which is not available in the input, and so they put greater emphasis on innate principles of language which learners can draw on.

Researchers and educators who are hoping for language acquisition theories which give them insight into language teaching practice are often frustrated by the lack of agreement among the 'experts'. But the complexities of SLA, like those of first language acquisition, represent a puzzle for linguistic, psychological, and neurological scientists which will not soon be solved. Research which has theory development as its goal has very important long-term significance for language teaching and learning, but agreement on a 'complete' theory of language acquisition is probably, at best, a long way off. Even if such agreement were reached, there would still be questions about how the theory should be interpreted for language teaching. Many teachers watch theory development with interest, but must continue to teach and plan lessons and assess students' performance in the absence of a comprehensive theory of second language learning.

There is a growing body of 'applied' research being carried out within these different theoretical frameworks, as well as others. This often starts from observations of second language acquisition, in both 'natural' or 'instructional' settings. The research draws on a wide range of theoretical orientations, sometimes explicitly stated, sometimes merely implied. It may provide a more immediately accessible basis for teachers' reflections about teaching. In the following chapters, we will look at research which has sought to explain the processes and outcomes of second language acquisition in a variety of settings.

Sources and suggestions for further reading

Overviews of theories of second language acquisition

Cook, V. 1991. *Second Language Learning and Language Teaching.* London: Edward Arnold.

Ellis, R. 1994. *The Study of Second Language Acquisition.* Oxford: Oxford University Press.

Ellis, R. 1997. *Second Language Acquisition.* Oxford: Oxford University Press.

Larsen-Freeman, D. and **M. H. Long.** 1991. *An Introduction to Second Language Acquisition Research.* New York: Longman.

Ritchie, W. C. and **T. K. Bhatia** (eds.). 1996. *Handbook of Second Language Acquisition.* San Diego, Cal.: Academic Press.

Skehan, P. 1998. *A Cognitive Approach to Language Learning.* Oxford: Oxford University Press.

Behaviourism in SLA

Lado, R. 1964. *Language Teaching: A Scientific Approach.* New York: McGraw-Hill.

Universal Grammar approaches to SLA

Gass, S. M. and **J. Schachter** (eds.). 1989. *Linguistic Perspectives on Second Language Acquisition.* Cambridge: Cambridge University Press.

Schwartz, B. 1993. 'On explicit and negative data effecting and affecting competence and linguistic behavior.' *Studies in Second Language Acquisition* 15: 147–63.

White, L. 1989. *Universal Grammar and Second Language Acquisition.* Amsterdam/Philadelphia, Pa.: John Benjamins.

Krashen's theory

Krashen, S. D. 1982. *Principles and Practice in Second Language Acquisition.* Oxford: Pergamon.

Krashen, S. D. 1985. *The Input Hypothesis.* London: Longman.

Krashen, S. D. and **T. Terrell.** 1983. *The Natural Approach: Language Acquisition in the Classroom.* Oxford: Pergamon.

Information processing

Bialystok, E. and **E. Ryan.** 1985. 'A metacognitive framework for the development of first and second language skills' in D. Forrest-Pressley, G. Mackinnon, and T. Waller (eds.): *Metacognition, Cognition, and Human Performance*, Vol. 12. New York: Academic Press, pp. 207–52.

McLaughlin, B. 1987. *Theories of Second Language Learning.* London: Edward Arnold.

Schmidt, R. 1990. 'The role of consciousness in second language learning.' *Applied Linguistics* 11: 17–46.

Connectionism

Ellis, N. C. and **R. Schmidt.** 1997. 'Morphology and longer distance dependencies.' *Studies in Second Language Acquisition* 19: 145–71.

Gasser, M. 1990. 'Connectionism and universals of second language acquisition.' *Studies in Second Language Acquisition* 12: 179–99.

Interactionism in SLA

Day, R. R. 1986. *Talking to Learn.* Rowley, Mass.: Newbury House.

Donato, R. 1994. 'Collective scaffolding in second language learning' in J. Lantolf and G. Appel (eds.): *Vygotskian Approaches to Second Language Research.* Norwood, N.J.: Ablex, pp. 33–56.

Gass, S. and **E. Varonis.** 1994. 'Input, interaction and second language production.' *Studies in Second Language Acquisition* 16: 283–302.

Hatch, E. 1992. *Discourse and Language Education.* Cambridge: Cambridge University Press.

Lantolf, J. P. and **G. Appel.** 1994. *Vygotskian Approaches to Second Language Research.* Norwood, N.J.: Ablex.

Long, M. H. 1983. 'Native speaker/non-native speaker conversation and the negotiation of comprehensible input.' *Applied Linguistics* 4: 126–41.

Pica, T. 1994. 'Research on negotiation: What does it reveal about second language acquisition? Conditions, processes, and outcomes.' *Language Learning* 44: 493–527.

3 FACTORS AFFECTING SECOND LANGUAGE LEARNING

In Chapter 1, it was pointed out that all normal children, given a normal upbringing, are successful in the acquisition of their first language. This contrasts with our experience of second language learners, whose success varies greatly.

Many of us believe that learners have certain characteristics which lead to more or less successful language learning. Such beliefs are usually based on anecdotal evidence, often our own experience or that of individual people we have known. For example, many teachers are convinced that extroverted learners who interact without inhibition in their second language and find many opportunities to practise language skills will be the most successful learners. In addition to personality characteristics, other factors generally considered to be relevant to language learning are intelligence, aptitude, motivation, and attitudes. Another important factor, as suggested in our discussion of the Critical Period Hypothesis for first language acquisition, is the age at which learning begins.

In this chapter, we will see whether anecdotal evidence is supported by research findings. To what extent can we predict differences in the success of second language acquisition in two individuals if we have information about their personalities, their general and specific intellectual abilities, their motivation, or their age?

Activity

Characteristics of the 'good language learner'

It seems that some people have a much easier time of learning than others. Rate of development varies widely among first language learners. Some children can string together five-, six-, and seven-word sentences at an age when other children are just beginning to label items in their immediate environment. Nevertheless, all normal children eventually master their first language.

In second language learning, it has been observed countless times that, in the same classroom setting, some students progress rapidly through the initial stages of learning a new language while others struggle along making very slow progress. Some learners never achieve *native-like* command of a second language. Are there personal characteristics that make one learner more successful than another, and if so, what are they?

The following is a list of some of the characteristics commonly thought to contribute to successful language learning. In your experience – as a second language learner and as a teacher – which characteristics seem to you most likely to be associated with success in second language acquisition in the classroom? Which ones would you be less inclined to expect in a successful learner?

In each case rate the characteristic as follows:

    1 = Very important
    2 = Quite important
    3 = Important
    4 = Not very important
    5 = Not at all important.

A good language learner:

a	is a willing and accurate guesser	1	2	3	4	5
b	tries to get a message across even if specific language knowledge is lacking	1	2	3	4	5
c	is willing to make mistakes	1	2	3	4	5
d	constantly looks for patterns in the language	1	2	3	4	5
e	practises as often as possible	1	2	3	4	5
f	analyses his or her own speech and the speech of others	1	2	3	4	5
g	attends to whether his or her performance meets the standards he or she has learned	1	2	3	4	5
h	enjoys grammar exercises	1	2	3	4	5
i	begins learning in childhood	1	2	3	4	5
j	has an above-average IQ	1	2	3	4	5
k	has good academic skills	1	2	3	4	5
l	has a good self-image and lots of confidence	1	2	3	4	5

All of the characteristics listed above can be classified into five main categories: motivation, aptitude, personality, intelligence, and learner preferences. However, many of the characteristics cannot be assigned exclusively to one category. For example, the characteristic 'is willing to make mistakes' can be considered a personality and/or a motivational factor if the learner is willing to make mistakes in order to get the message across.

Research on learner characteristics

Perhaps the best way to begin our discussion is to describe how research on the influence of learner characteristics on second language learning has been carried out. When researchers are interested in finding out whether an individual factor such as motivation affects second language learning, they usually select a group of learners and give them a questionnaire to measure the type and degree of their motivation. The learners are then given a test to measure their second language proficiency. The test and the questionnaire are both scored and the researcher performs a *correlation* on the two measures, to see whether learners with high scores on the proficiency test are also more likely to have high scores on the motivation questionnaire. If this is the case, the researcher concludes that high levels of motivation are correlated with success in language learning. A similar procedure can be used to assess the relationship between intelligence and second language acquisition through the use of IQ tests.

Although this procedure seems straightforward, there are several difficulties with it. The first problem is that it is not possible to directly observe and measure qualities such as motivation, extroversion, or even intelligence. These are just labels for an entire range of behaviours and characteristics. Furthermore, because characteristics such as these are not independent, it will come as no surprise that different researchers have often used the same labels to describe different sets of behavioural traits.

For example, in motivation questionnaires, learners are often asked whether they willingly seek out opportunities to use their second language with native speakers and if so, how often they do this. The assumption behind such a question is that learners who report that they often seek out opportunities to interact with speakers of the second language are highly motivated to learn. Although this assumption seems reasonable, it is problematic because if a learner responds by saying 'yes' to this question, we may assume that the learner has more opportunities for language practice in informal contexts. Because it is usually impossible to separate these two factors (i.e. willingness to interact and opportunities to interact), some researchers have been criticized for concluding that it is the motivation rather than the opportunity which makes the greater contribution to success.

Another factor which makes it difficult to reach conclusions about relationships between individual learner characteristics and second language learning is how language proficiency is defined and measured. To illustrate this point let us refer once again to 'motivation'. In the second language learning literature, some studies report that learners with a higher level of motivation are more successful language learners than those with lower motivation, while other studies report that highly motivated learners do not perform any better on a proficiency test than learners with much less motivation to learn the second language. One explanation which has been offered for these conflicting findings is that the language proficiency tests used in different studies do not measure the same kind of knowledge. That is, in informal language learning settings, highly motivated learners may be more successful when the proficiency tests measure oral communication skills. In other studies, however, highly motivated learners may not be more successful because the tests are primarily measures of metalinguistic knowledge. Results such as these imply that motivation to learn a second language may be more related to particular aspects of language proficiency than to others.

Finally, there is the problem of interpreting the correlation of two factors as being due to a causal relationship between them. That is, the fact that two things tend to occur together does not necessarily mean that one caused the other. While it may be that that one factor influences the other, it may also be the case that both are influenced by something else entirely. Research on motivation is perhaps the best context in which to illustrate this. Learners who are successful may indeed be highly motivated. But can we conclude that they became successful because of their motivation? It is also plausible that early success heightened their motivation or that both success and motivation are due to their special aptitude for language learning or the favourable context in which they are learning.

Intelligence

The term 'intelligence' has traditionally been used to refer to performance on certain kinds of tests. These tests are often associated with success in school, and a link between intelligence and second language learning has sometimes been reported. Over the years, many studies using a variety of intelligence ('IQ') tests and different methods of assessing language learning have found that IQ scores were a good means of predicting how successful a learner would be. Some recent studies have shown that these measures of intelligence may be more strongly related to certain kinds of second language abilities than to others. For example, in a study with French *immersion* students in Canada, it was found that, while intelligence was related to the development of French second language reading, grammar, and vocabulary, it was unrelated to oral productive skills (Genesee 1976). Similar findings have been reported in other studies. What this suggests is that, while intelligence, especially as measured by verbal IQ tests, may be a strong factor when it comes to learning which involves language analysis and rule learning, intelligence may play a less important role in classrooms where the instruction focuses more on communication and interaction.

It is important to keep in mind that 'intelligence' is complex and that individuals have many kinds of abilities and strengths, not all of which are measured by traditional IQ tests. In our experience, many students whose academic performance has been weak have experienced considerable success in second language learning.

Aptitude

There is evidence in the research literature that some individuals have an exceptional 'aptitude' for language learning. Lorraine Obler (1989) reports that a man, whom she calls CJ, has such a specialized ability. CJ is a native speaker of English who grew up in an English home. His first true experience with a second language came at the age of 15 when he began learning French in school. CJ also studied German, Spanish, and Latin while in high school. At age 20, he made a brief visit to Germany. CJ reported that just hearing German spoken for a short time was enough for him to 'recover' the German he had learned in school. Later, CJ worked in Morocco where he reported learning Moroccan Arabic through both formal instruction and informal immersion. He also spent some time in Spain and Italy, where he apparently 'picked up' both Spanish and Italian in a 'matter of weeks'. A remarkable talent indeed!

Learning quickly is the distinguishing feature of aptitude. The 'aptitude' factor has been investigated most intensively by researchers interested in developing tests which can be used to predict whether individuals will be efficient learners of a foreign language in a classroom setting. The most widely used aptitude tests are the Modern Language Aptitude Test (MLAT) and the Pimsleur Language Aptitude Battery (PLAB). Both tests are based on the view that aptitude is composed of different types of abilities:

(1) the ability to identify and memorize new sounds; (2) the ability to understand the function of particular words in sentences; (3) the ability to figure out grammatical rules from language samples; and (4) memory for new words. While earlier research revealed a substantial relationship between performance on the MLAT or PLAB and performance in foreign language learning, these studies were conducted at a time when second language teaching was based on *grammar translation* or *audiolingual* methods (see Chapter 5). With the adoption of a more communicative approach to teaching, many teachers and researchers came to see aptitude as irrelevant to

the process of language acquisition. Unfortunately, this means that relatively little research has actually explored whether having a skill such as the 'ability to identify and memorize new sounds' is advantageous when classroom instruction is meaning-oriented rather than focused on drills or metalinguistic explanations.

Successful language learners may not be strong in all of the components of aptitude. Some individuals may have strong memories but only average abilities in the other components of aptitude. Ideally, one could determine learners' profiles of strengths and weaknesses and use this information to place students in appropriate teaching programs. An example of how this can be done is described by Marjorie Wesche (1981). In a Canadian language program for adult learners of French, students were placed in an instructional program which was compatible with their aptitude profile and information about their learning experiences. Students who were high on analytic ability, but average on memory, were assigned to teaching that focused on grammàtical structures, while learners strong in memory but average on analytic skills were placed in a class where the teaching was organized around the functional use of the second language in specific situations. Wesche reported a high level of student and teacher satisfaction when students were matched with compatible teaching environments. In addition, some evidence indicated that matched students were able to attain significantly higher levels of achievement than those who were unmatched.

While few second language teaching contexts are able to offer such choices to their students, teachers may find that knowing the aptitude profile of their students will help them in selecting appropriate classroom activities for particular groups of students. Or, if they do not have such information, they may wish to ensure that their teaching activities are sufficiently varied to accommodate learners with different aptitude profiles.

Personality

A number of personality characteristics have been proposed as likely to affect second language learning, but it has not been easy to demonstrate their effects in empirical studies. As with other research investigating the effects of individual characteristics on second language learning, different studies measuring a similar personality trait produce different results. For example, it is often argued that an extroverted person is well suited to language learning. However, research does not always support this conclusion. Although some studies have found that success in language learning is correlated with learners' scores on characteristics often associated with extroversion such as assertiveness and adventurousness, others have found that many successful language learners do not get high scores on measures of extroversion.

Another aspect of personality which has been studied is inhibition. It has been suggested that inhibition discourages risk-taking which is necessary for progress in language learning. This is often considered to be a particular problem for adolescents, who are more self-conscious than younger learners. In a series of studies, Alexander Guiora and his colleagues found support for the claim that inhibition is a negative force, at least for second language pronunciation performance. One study involved an analysis of the effects of small doses of alcohol on pronunciation (Guiora *et al.* 1972). They found that subjects who received small doses of alcohol did better on pronunciation tests than those who did not drink any alcohol. While results such as these are interesting, as well as amusing, they are not completely convincing, since the experiments are far removed from the reality of the classroom situation. Furthermore, they may have more to do with performance than with learning. We may also note, in passing, that when larger doses of alcohol were administered, pronunciation rapidly deteriorated!

Several other personality characteristics such as self-esteem, empathy, dominance, talkativeness, and responsiveness have also been studied. However, in general, the available research does not show a clearly defined relationship between personality and second language acquisition. And, as indicated earlier, the major difficulty in investigating personality characteristics is that of identification and measurement. Another explanation which has been offered for the mixed findings of personality studies is that personality variables may be a major factor only in the acquisition of conversational skills, not in the acquisition of literacy skills. The confused picture of the research on personality factors may be due in part to the fact that comparisons are made between studies that measure communicative ability and studies that measure grammatical accuracy or metalinguistic knowledge. Personality variables seem to be consistently related to the former, but not to the latter.

Despite the contradictory results and the problems involved in carrying out research in the area of personality characteristics, many researchers believe that personality will be shown to have an important influence on success in language learning. This relationship is a complex one, however, in that it is probably not personality alone, but the way in which it combines with other factors, that contributes to second language learning.

Motivation and attitudes

There has been a great deal of research on the role of attitudes and motivation in second language learning. The overall findings show that positive attitudes and motivation are related to success in second language learning (Gardner 1985). Unfortunately, the research cannot indicate precisely *how* motivation is related to learning. As indicated above, we do not know whether it is the motivation that produces successful learning or successful learning that enhances motivation or whether both are affected by other factors. As noted by Peter Skehan (1989), the question is, are learners more highly motivated because they are successful, or are they successful because they are highly motivated?

Motivation in second language learning is a complex phenomenon which can be defined in terms of two factors: learners' communicative needs and their attitudes towards the second language community. If learners need to speak the second language in a wide range of social situations or to fulfil professional ambitions, they will perceive the communicative value of the second language and will therefore be motivated to acquire proficiency in it. Likewise, if learners have favourable attitudes towards the speakers of the language, they will desire more contact with them. Robert Gardner and Wallace Lambert (1972) coined the terms *integrative motivation* to refer to language learning for personal growth and cultural enrichment, and *instrumental motivation* for language learning for more immediate or practical goals. Research has shown that these types of motivation are related to success in second language learning.

On the other hand, we should keep in mind that an individual's identity is closely linked with the way he or she speaks. It follows that when speaking a new language one is adopting some of the identity markers of another cultural group. Depending on the learner's attitudes, learning a second language can be a source of enrichment or a source of resentment. If the speaker's only reason for learning the second language is external pressure, internal motivation may be minimal and general attitudes towards learning may be negative.

One factor which often affects motivation is the social dynamic or power relationship between the languages. That is, members of a minority group learning the language of a majority group may have different attitudes and motivation from those of majority group members learning a minority language. Even though it is impossible to predict the exact effect of such societal factors on second language learning, the fact that languages exist in social contexts cannot be overlooked when we seek to understand the variables which affect success in learning. Children as well as adults are sensitive to social dynamics and power relationships.

Motivation in the classroom setting

In a teacher's mind, motivated students are usually those who participate actively in class, express interest in the subject-matter, and study a great deal. Teachers can easily recognize characteristics such as these. They also have more opportunity to influence these characteristics than students' reasons for studying the second language or their attitudes toward the language and its speakers. If we can make our classrooms places where students enjoy coming because the content is interesting and relevant to their age and level of ability, where the learning goals are challenging yet manageable and clear, and where the atmosphere is supportive and non-threatening, we can make a positive contribution to students' motivation to learn.

Although little research has been done to investigate how pedagogy interacts with motivation in second language classrooms, considerable work has been done within the field of educational psychology. In a review of some of this work, Graham Crookes and Richard Schmidt (1991) point to several areas where educational research has reported increased levels of motivation for students in relation to pedagogical practices. Included among these are:

Motivating students into the lesson At the opening stages of lessons (and within transitions), it has been observed that remarks teachers make about forthcoming activities can lead to higher levels of interest on the part of the students.

Varying the activities, tasks, and materials Students are reassured by the existence of classroom routines which they can depend on. However, lessons which always consist of the same routines, patterns, and formats have been shown to lead to a decrease in attention and an increase in boredom. Varying the activities, tasks, and materials can help to avoid this and increase students' interest levels.

Using co-operative rather than competitive goals Co-operative learning activities are those in which students must work together in order to complete a task or solve a problem. These techniques have been found to increase the self-confidence of students, including weaker ones, because every participant in a co-operative task has an important role to play. Knowing that their team-mates are counting on them can increase students' motivation.

Clearly, cultural and age differences will determine the most appropriate way for teachers to motivate students. In some classrooms, students may thrive on competitive interaction, while in others, co-operative activities will be more successful.

Learner preferences

Learners have clear preferences for how they go about learning new material. The term 'learning style' has been used to describe an individual's natural, habitual, and preferred way of absorbing, processing, and retaining new information and skills (Reid 1995). We have all heard people say that they cannot learn something until they have seen it. Such learners would fall into the group called 'visual' learners. Other people, who may be called 'aural' learners, seem to need only to hear something once or twice before they know it. For others, who are referred to as 'kinaesthetic' learners, there is a need to add a physical action to the learning process. In contrast to these perceptually based learning styles, considerable research has focused on a cognitive learning style distinction between *field independent* and *field dependent* learners. This refers to whether an individual tends to separate details from the general background or to see things more holistically. Another category of learning styles is based on the individual's temperament or personality.

While recent years have seen the development of many learning style assessment instruments, very little research has examined the interaction between different learning styles and success in second language acquisition. At present, the only learning style that has been extensively investigated is the field independence/dependence distinction. The results from this research have shown that while field independence is related to some degree to performance on certain kinds of tasks, it is not a good predictor of performance on others.

Although there is a need for considerably more research on learning styles, when learners express a preference for seeing something written or for memorizing material which we feel should be learned in a less formal way, we should not assume that their ways of working are wrong. Instead, we should encourage them to use all means available to them as they work to learn another language. At a minimum, research on learning styles should make us sceptical of claims that a particular teaching method or textbook will suit the needs of all learners.

Learner beliefs

Second language learners are not always conscious of their individual learning styles, but virtually all learners, particularly older learners, have strong beliefs and opinions about how their instruction should be delivered. These beliefs are usually based on previous learning experiences and the assumption (right or wrong) that a particular type of instruction is the best way for them to learn. This is another area where little work has been done. However, the available research indicates that learner beliefs can be strong mediating factors in their experience in the classroom. For example, in a survey of international students learning ESL in a highly communicative program at an English-speaking university, Carlos Yorio (1986) found high levels of dissatisfaction among the students. The type of communicative instruction they received focused exclusively on meaning and spontaneous communication in group-work interaction. In their responses to a questionnaire, the majority of students expressed concerns about several aspects of their instruction, most notably, the absence of attention to language form, corrective feedback, or teacher-centred instruction. Although this study did not directly examine learners' progress in relation to their opinions about the instruction they received, several of them were convinced that their progress was negatively affected by an instructional approach which was not consistent with their beliefs about the best ways for them to learn.

Learners' preferences for learning, whether due to their learning style or to their beliefs about how languages are learned, will influence the kinds of strategies they choose in order to learn new material. Teachers can use this information to help learners expand their repertoire of learning strategies and thus develop greater flexibility in their ways of approaching language learning.

Age of acquisition

We now turn to a learner characteristic of a different type: age. This characteristic is easier to define and measure than personality, aptitude, or motivation. Nevertheless, the relationship between a learner's age and his or her potential for success in second language acquisition is the subject of much lively debate.

It has been widely observed that children from immigrant families eventually speak the language of their new community with native-like fluency, but their parents rarely achieve such high levels of mastery of the spoken language. To be sure, there are cases where adult second language learners have distinguished themselves by their exceptional performance. For example, one often sees reference to Joseph Conrad, a native speaker of Polish who became a major writer in the English language. Many adult second language learners become capable of communicating very successfully in the language but, for most, differences of accent, word choice, or grammatical features distinguish them from native speakers and from second language speakers who began learning the language while they were very young.

One explanation for this difference is that, as in first language acquisition, there is a critical period for second language acquisition. As discussed in Chapter 1, the Critical Period Hypothesis suggests that there is a time in human development when the brain is predisposed for success in language learning. Developmental changes in the brain, it is argued, affect the nature of language acquisition. According to this view, language learning which occurs after the end of the critical period may not be based on the innate biological structures believed to contribute to first language acquisition or second language acquisition in early childhood. Rather, older learners depend on more general learning abilities – the same ones they might use to learn other kinds of skills or information. It is argued that these general learning abilities are not as successful for language learning as the more specific, innate capacities which are available to the young child. It is most often claimed that the critical period ends somewhere around puberty, but some researchers suggest it could be even earlier.

Of course, as we saw in Chapter 2, it is difficult to compare children and adults as second language learners. In addition to the possible biological differences suggested by the Critical Period Hypothesis, the conditions for language learning are often very different. Younger learners in informal language learning environments usually have more time to devote to learning language. They often have more opportunities to hear and use the language in environments where they do not experience strong pressure to speak fluently and accurately from the very beginning. Furthermore, their early imperfect efforts are often praised or, at least, accepted. On the other hand, older learners are often in situations which demand much more complex language and the expression of much more complicated ideas. Adults are often embarrassed by their lack of mastery of the language and they may develop a sense of inadequacy after experiences of frustration in trying to say exactly what they mean.

The Critical Period Hypothesis has been challenged in recent years from several different points of view. Some studies of the second language development of older and younger learners who are learning in similar circumstances have shown that, at least in the early stages of second language development, older learners are more efficient than younger learners. In educational research, it has been reported that learners who began learning a second language at the primary school level did not fare better in the long run than those who began in early adolescence. Furthermore, there are countless anecdotes about older learners (adolescents and adults) who have reached high levels of proficiency in a second language. Does this mean that there is no critical period for second language acquisition?

In the following pages, we will review some studies designed to investigate the Critical Period Hypothesis as it relates to second language learning.

Critical Period Hypothesis: More than just accent?

Most studies of the relationship between age of acquisition and second language development have focused on learners' phonological (pronunciation) achievement. In general, these studies have concluded that older learners almost inevitably have a noticeable 'foreign accent'. But what of other linguistic features? Is syntax (word order, overall sentence structure) as dependent on age of acquisition as phonological development? What about morphology (for example, grammatical morphemes which mark such things as verb tense or the number and gender of nouns)? One study that attempted to answer these questions was done by Mark Patkowski (1980).

Mastery of the spoken language
Mark Patkowski studied the effect of age on the acquisition of features of a second language other than accent. He hypothesized that, even if accent were ignored, only those who had begun learning their second language before the age of 15 could ever achieve full, native-like mastery of that language. Patkowski examined the spoken English of 67 highly educated immigrants to the United States. They had started to learn English at various ages, but all had lived in the United States for more than five years. The spoken English of 15 native-born Americans English speakers from a similarly high level of education served as a sort of baseline of what the second language learners might be trying to attain as the target language. Inclusion of the native speakers also provided evidence concerning the validity of the research procedures.

A lengthy interview with each of the subjects in the study was tape recorded. Because Patkowski wanted to remove the possibility that the results would be affected by accent, he did not ask the raters to judge the tape-recorded interviews themselves. Instead, he transcribed five-minute samples from the interviews. These samples (from which any identifying or revealing information about immigration history had been removed) were rated by trained native-speaker judges. The judges were asked to place each speaker on a rating scale from 0, representing no knowledge of the language, to 5, representing a level of English expected from an educated native speaker.

The main question in Patkowski's research was: 'Will there be a difference between learners who began to learn English before puberty and those who began learning English later?' However, in the light of some of the issues discussed above, he also compared learners on the basis of other characteristics and experiences which some people have suggested might be as good as age in predicting or explaining a learner's eventual success in mastering a second language. For example, he looked at the relationship between eventual mastery and the total amount of time a speaker had been in the United States as well as the amount of formal ESL instruction each speaker had had.

The findings were quite dramatic. Thirty-two out of 33 subjects who had begun learning English before the age of 15 scored at the 4+ or the 5 level. The homogeneity of the pre-puberty learners seemed to suggest that, for this group, success in learning a second language was almost inevitable (see Figure 3.1). On the other hand, there was much more variety in the levels achieved by the post-puberty group. The majority of the post-puberty learners centred around the 3+ level, but there was a wide distribution of levels achieved. This variety made the performance of this group look more like the sort of performance range one would expect if one were measuring success in learning almost any kind of skill or knowledge.

Patkowski's first question, 'Will there be a difference between learners who began to learn English before puberty and those who began learning English later?', was answered with a very resounding 'yes'. When he examined the other factors which might be thought to affect success in second language acquisition, the picture was much less clear. There was, naturally, some relationship between these other factors and learning success. However, it often turned out that age was so closely related to the other factors that it was not really possible to separate them completely. For example, length of residence in the United States sometimes seemed to be a fairly good predictor. However, while it was true that a person who had lived in the country for 15 years might speak better than one who had been there for only 10 years, it was often the case that the one with longer residence had also arrived at an earlier age. However, a person who had arrived in the United States at the age of 18 and had lived there for 20 years did not score significantly better than someone who had arrived at the age of 18 but had only lived there for 10 years. Similarly, amount of instruction, when separated from age, did not predict success to the extent that age of immigration did.

Thus, Patkowski found that age of acquisition is a very important factor in setting limits on the development of native-like mastery of a second language and that this limitation does not apply only to accent. These results gave added support to the Critical Period Hypothesis for second language acquisition.

Figure 3.1: Bar charts showing the language levels of pre- and post-puberty learners of English (Patkowski 1980).

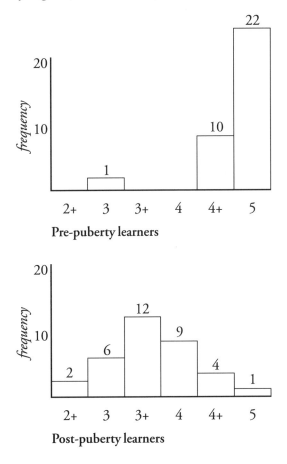

Pre-puberty learners

Post-puberty learners

Experience and research have shown that native-like mastery of the spoken language is difficult to attain by older learners. Surprisingly, even the ability to distinguish between grammatical and ungrammatical sentences in a second language appears to be affected by the age factor, as we will see in the next study by Johnson and Newport.

Intuitions of grammaticality

Jacqueline Johnson and Elissa Newport conducted a study of 46 Chinese and Korean speakers who had begun to learn English at different ages. All subjects were students or faculty at an American university and all had been in the United States for at least three years. The study also included 23 native speakers of English (Johnson and Newport 1989).

The participants in the study were given a judgement of grammaticality task which tested 12 rules of English morphology and syntax. They heard sentences on a tape and had to indicate whether or not each sentence was correct. Half of the sentences were grammatical, half were not.

When they scored the tests, Johnson and Newport found that age of arrival in the United States was a significant predictor of success on the test. When they grouped the learners in the same way as Patkowski, comparing those who began their intensive exposure to English between the ages of 3 and 15 with those who arrived in the United States between the ages of 17 and 39, once again they found that there was a strong relationship between an early start to language learning and better performance in the second language. Johnson and Newport noted that for those who began before the age of 15, and especially before the age of 10, there were few individual differences in second language ability. Those who began later did not have native-like language abilities and were more likely to differ greatly from one another in ultimate attainment.

This study, then, further supports the hypothesis that there is a critical period for attaining full native-like mastery of a second language. Nevertheless, there is some research which suggests that older learners may have an advantage, at least in the early stages of second language learning.

Is younger really better?

In 1978, Catherine Snow and Marian Hoefnagel-Höhle published an article based on a research project they had carried out in Holland. They had studied the progress of a group of English speakers who were learning Dutch as a second language. What made their research especially valuable was that the learners they were following included children as young as three years old as well as older children, adolescents, and adults. Furthermore, a large number of tasks was used, to measure different types of language use and language knowledge.

Pronunciation was tested by having learners pronounce 80 Dutch words twice: the first time immediately after hearing a native speaker say the word; the second time, a few minutes later, they were asked to say the word represented in a picture, without a model to imitate. Tape recordings of the learners were rated by a native speaker of Dutch on a six-point scale.

In an *auditory discrimination* test, learners saw pictures of four objects. In each group of four there were two whose names formed a minimal pair, that is, alike except for one sound (an example in English would be 'ship' and 'sheep'). Learners heard one of the words and were asked to indicate which picture was named by the word they heard.

Morphology was tested using a procedure like the 'wug test', which required learners to complete sentences by adding the correct grammatical markers to words which were supplied by the researchers. Again, to take an example from English, learners were asked to complete sentences such as 'Here is one boy. Now there are two of them. There are two _____ .'

The *sentence repetition* task required learners to repeat 37 sentences of increasing length and grammatical complexity.

For *sentence translation*, learners were given 60 sentences to translate from English to Dutch. A point was given for each grammatical structure which was rendered into the correct Dutch equivalent.

In the *sentence judgement task*, learners were to judge which of two sentences was better. The same content was expressed in both sentences, but one sentence was grammatically correct while the other contained errors.

In the *Peabody Picture Vocabulary Test*, learners saw four pictures and heard one isolated word. Their task was to indicate which picture matched the word spoken by the tester.

For the *story comprehension task*, learners heard a story in Dutch and were then asked to retell the story in English or Dutch (according to their preference).

Finally, *the storytelling task* required learners to tell a story in Dutch, using a set of pictures they were given. Rate of delivery of speech mattered more than the expression of content or formal accuracy.

The learners were divided into several age groups, but for our discussion we will divide them into just three groups: children (aged 3 to 10), adolescents (12 to 15 years), and adults (18 to 60 years). The children and adolescents all attended Dutch schools. Some of the adults worked in Dutch work environments, but most of their Dutch colleagues spoke English well. Other adults were parents who did not work outside their homes and thus had somewhat less contact with Dutch than most of the other subjects.

The learners were tested three times, at four- to five-month intervals. They were first tested within six months of their arrival in Holland and within six weeks of their starting school or work in a Dutch-language environment.

Activity

Comparing child, adolescent, and adult language learners

Which group do you think did best on the first test (that is, who learned fastest)? Which group do you think was best by the end of the year? Do you think some groups would do better on certain tasks than others? For example, who do you think would do best on the pronunciation tasks, and who would do best on the tasks requiring more metalinguistic awareness? Compare your predictions with the results for the different tasks which are presented in Table 3.1. An 'X' indicates that the group was the best on the test at the beginning of the year (an indication of the rate of learning), and a 'Y' indicates the group that did best at the end of the year (an indication of eventual attainment).

Table 3.1: Comparison of language learning at different ages

Task	Child	Adolescent	Adult
Pronunciation	Y	Y	X
Auditory discrimination		XY	
Morphology		XY	
Sentence repetition		XY	
Sentence translation	*	XY	
Sentence judgement	*	XY	
Peabody picture vocabulary test		XY	
Story comprehension	Y	X	
Storytelling	Y	X	

* These tests were too difficult for child learners.

In the Snow and Hoefnagel-Höhle study, the adolescents were by far the most successful learners. They were ahead of everyone on all but one of the tests (pronunciation) on the first test session. That is, within the first few months the adolescents had already made the most progress in learning Dutch. As the table indicates, it was the adults who were better than the children and adolescents on pronunciation in the first test session. Surprisingly, it was also the adults, not the children, whose scores were second best on the other tests at the first test session. In other words, adolescents and adults learned faster than children in the first few months of exposure to Dutch.

By the end of the year, the children were catching up, or had surpassed, the adults on several measures. Nevertheless, it was the adolescents who retained the highest levels of performance overall.

Snow and Hoefnagel-Höhle concluded that their results provide evidence that there is no critical period for language acquisition. However, their results can be interpreted in some other ways as well:

1 Some of the tasks, (for example, sentence judgement or translation) were too hard for young learners. Even in their native language, these tasks would have been unfamiliar and difficult. In fact, young Dutch native speakers to whom the second language learners were compared also had trouble with these tasks.

2 Adults and adolescents may learn faster in the early stages of second language development (especially if they are learning a language which is similar to their first language). Young children eventually catch up and even surpass them if their exposure to the language takes place in contexts where they are surrounded by the language on a daily basis.

3 Adults and adolescents can make considerable and rapid progress towards mastery of a second language in contexts where they can make use of the language on a daily basis in social, personal, professional, or academic interaction.

At what age should second language instruction begin?

Even people who know nothing about the critical period research are certain that, in school programs for second or foreign language teaching, 'younger is better'. However, both experience and research show that older learners can attain high, if not 'native', levels of proficiency in their second language. Furthermore, it is essential to think carefully about the goals of an instructional program and the context in which it occurs before we jump to conclusions about the necessity – or even the desirability – of the earliest possible start.

The role of the critical period in second language acquisition is still much debated. For every researcher who holds that there are maturational constraints on language acquisition, there is another who considers that the age factor cannot be separated from factors such as motivation, social identity, and the conditions for learning. They argue that older learners may well speak with an accent because they want to continue being identified with their first language cultural group, and adults rarely get access to the same quantity and quality of language input that children receive in play settings.

Many people conclude on the basis of studies such as those by Patkowski or Newport and Johnson that it is better to begin second language instruction as early as possible. Yet it is very important to bear in mind the context of these studies. They deal with the highest possible level of second language skills, the level at which a second language speaker is indistinguishable from a native speaker. But achieving a native-like mastery of the second language is not a goal for all second language learning, in all contexts.

When the objective of second language learning is native-like mastery of the target language, it is usually desirable for the learner to be completely surrounded by the language as early as possible. However, as we saw in Chapter 1, early intensive exposure to the second language may entail the loss or incomplete development of the child's first language.

When the goal is basic communicative ability for all students in a school setting, and when it is assumed that the child's native language will remain the primary language, it may be more efficient to begin second or *foreign language* teaching later. When learners receive only a few hours of instruction per week, learners who start later (for example, at age 10, 11, or 12) often catch up with those who began earlier. We have often seen second or foreign language programs which begin with very young learners but offer only minimal contact with the language. Even when students do make progress in these early-start programs, they sometimes find themselves placed in secondary school classes with students who have had no previous instruction. After years of classes, learners feel frustrated by the lack of progress, and their motivation to continue may be diminished. School programs should be based on realistic estimates of how long it takes to learn a second language. One or two hours a week will not produce very advanced second language speakers, no matter how young they were when they began.

Summary

The learner's age is one of the characteristics which determine the way in which an individual approaches second language learning. But the opportunities for learning (both inside and outside the classroom), the motivation to learn, and individual differences in aptitude for language learning are also important determining factors in both rate of learning and eventual success in learning.

In this chapter, we have looked at the ways in which intelligence, aptitude, personality and motivational characteristics, learner preferences, and age have been found to influence second language learning. We have learned that the study of individual learner variables is not easy and that the results of research are not entirely satisfactory. This is partly because of the lack of clear definitions and methods for measuring the individual characteristics. It is also due to the fact that these learner characteristics are not independent of one another: learner variables interact in complex ways. So far, researchers know very little about the nature of these complex interactions. Thus, it remains difficult to make precise predictions about how a particular individual's characteristics influence his or her success as a language learner. Nonetheless, in a classroom, a sensitive teacher, who takes learners' individual personalities and learning styles into account, can create a learning environment in which virtually all learners can be successful in learning a second language.

Sources and suggestions for further reading

General discussion of individual differences

Naiman, N., M. Fröhlich, H. H. Stern, and **A. Todesco.** 1995. *The Good Language Learner.* Clevedon, UK: Multilingual Matters.

Skehan, P. 1991. 'Individual differences in second language learning.' *Studies in Second Language Acquisition* 13/2: 275–98.

Intelligence

Genesee, F. 1976. 'The role of intelligence in second language learning.' *Language Learning* 26/2: 267–80.

Aptitude

Skehan, P. 1989. *Individual Differences in Second Language Learning.* London: Edward Arnold.

The case of CJ

Obler, L. 1989. 'Exceptional second language learners' in S. Gass, C. Madden, D. Preston, and L. Selinker (eds.): *Variation in Second Language Acquisition, Vol. II: Psycholinguistic Issues.* Clevedon, UK/Philadelphia, Pa.: Multilingual Matters, pp. 141–59.

Motivation and attitudes

Crookes, G. and **R. Schmidt.** 1991. 'Motivation: "Reopening the research agenda".' *Language Learning* 41/4: 469–512.

Gardner, R. 1985. *Social Psychology and Second Language Learning: The Role of Attitudes and Motivation.* London: Edward Arnold.

Gardner, R. C. and **W. E. Lambert.** 1972. *Attitudes and Motivation in Second-Language Learning.* Rowley, Mass.: Newbury House.

Oxford, R. and **J. Shearin.** 1994. 'Language learning motivation: Expanding the theoretical framework.' *Modern Language Journal* 78/1: 12–28.

Inhibition and second language learning

Guiora, A., B. Beit-Hallahami, R. Brannon, C. Dull, and **T. Scovel.** 1972. 'The effects of experimentally induced changes in ego states on pronunciation ability in a second language: An exploratory study.' *Comprehensive Psychiatry* 13/5: 421–8.

Learner preferences

Reid, J. (ed.). 1995. *Learning Styles in the ESL/EFL Classroom.* New York: Heinle & Heinle.

Oxford, R. 1990. *Language Learning Strategies: What Every Teacher Should Know.* New York: Newbury House.

Wesche, M. B. 1981. 'Language aptitude measures in streaming, matching students with methods, and diagnosis of learning problems' in K. Diller (ed.): *Individual Differences and Universals in Language Learning Aptitude.* Rowley, Mass.: Newbury House. pp. 119–39.

Yorio, C. 1986. 'Consumerism in second language learning and teaching.' *Canadian Modern Language Review* 42/3: 668–87.

Age of acquisition

Burstall, C. 1975. 'French in the primary school: The British experiment.' *Canadian Modern Language Review* 31/5: 388–402.

Johnson, J. and **E. Newport.** 1989. 'Critical period effects in second language learning: The influence of maturational state on the acquisition of English as a second language.' *Cognitive Psychology* 21: 60–99.

Long, M. H. 1990. 'Maturational constraints on language development.' *Studies in Second Language Acquisition* 12/3: 251–85.

Patkowski, M. 1980. 'The sensitive period for the acquisition of syntax in a second language.' *Language Learning* 30/2: 449–72.

Scovel, T. 1988. *A Time to Speak: A Psycholinguistic Inquiry into the Critical Period for Human Speech.* Cambridge, Mass.: Newbury House.

Snow, C. and **M. Hoefnagel-Höhle.** 1978. 'The critical period for language acquisition: evidence from second language learning.' *Child Development* 49/4: 1114–28.

The importance of maintaining the first language

Cummins, J. 1984. *Bilingualism and Special Education: Issues in Assessment and Pedagogy.* Clevedon, UK: Multilingual Matters.

Wong-Fillmore, L. 1991. 'When learning a second language means losing the first.' *Early Childhood Research Quarterly* 6/3: 323–46.

4 LEARNER LANGUAGE

In this chapter we shift our attention away from learner characteristics to the learner's language itself. We examine the types of errors that learners make and discuss what their errors can tell us about their knowledge of the language and their ability to use that knowledge. We will also look at stages and sequences in the acquisition of particular linguistic forms, keeping in mind the role of first language influence in second language learning.

Knowing more about the development of learner language helps teachers to assess teaching procedures in the light of what they can reasonably expect to accomplish in the classroom. As we will see, there are some characteristics of learner language which can be quite perplexing if one does not have an overall picture of the steps learners go through in acquiring features of the second language.

In presenting some of the findings of SLA research, we have included a number of samples of learner language to illustrate the various research findings and to give you an opportunity to practise analysing learner language. Of course, teachers analyse learner language all the time. They try to determine whether their students have learned what has been taught and how closely their language matches the target language. But progress cannot always be measured in these terms. Sometimes movement from one point in a sequence of development to another can actually lead from apparently correct performance (sometimes based on rote learning or very limited knowledge) to incorrect performance (based on an emerging understanding of the underlying rules or grammatical relationships in the language being learned). Thus, an increase in error may be an indication of progress. A simple example of this is irregular verbs. Just like young children, second language learners usually learn the irregular past tense forms of certain verbs before they learn to apply the regular simple past *-ed* marker. That means that a learner who says 'I buyed a bus ticket' may know more about English grammar than one who says 'I bought a bus ticket.'

The concept of learner language

As we saw in Chapter 1, children do not learn language simply through imitation and practice. Instead, they produce sentences that are not like those they have heard. These sentences seem to be created on the basis of some internal processes and knowledge which interact with the language they hear, permitting them to discover the complexities of the adult language gradually. Children's early language seems best described as a developing system with its own interim structure, not simply as an imperfect imitation of adult sentences.

In Chapter 1 we also saw that children's knowledge of the grammatical system is built up in predictable sequences. For instance, grammatical morphemes such as the *-ing* of the present progressive or the *-ed* of the simple past are not acquired at the same time, but in sequence. Furthermore, the acquisition of certain grammatical features follows similar patterns in children in different environments. As children continue to hear and use their language, they are able to revise these systems in ways which gradually develop towards the system of an adult.

But what about second language learning? Does it evolve in similar ways? Do second language learners develop their own language system in much the same way as first language learners? How does instruction affect the language acquisition of learners who are exposed to the language mainly in a foreign language classroom?

Until the late 1960s, most people regarded second language learners' speech simply as an incorrect version of the target language. Their errors were believed to be the result mainly of transfer from their first language. Contrastive analysis was the basis for identifying differences between the first and second language and for predicting areas of potential error. So, for example, one might predict that a speaker of French would be likely to express the idea of being cold as 'I have cold' in English because this would be a direct translation of the way this meaning is expressed in French (*j'ai froid*). And, indeed, some errors of this type do occur in learners' language.

As we saw in Chapter 2, however, not all errors made by second language learners can be explained in terms of first language transfer alone. A number of studies show that many errors can be explained better in terms of learners' attempts to discover the structure of the language being learned rather than an attempt to transfer patterns of their first language. Furthermore, some of the errors are remarkably similar to the kinds of errors made by young first language learners. An example in English would be the use of a regular *-ed* past tense ending on an irregular verb (as in the example, 'I buyed a bus ticket').

In addition, it has been observed that the errors are not always 'bi-directional'. A traditional version of the Contrastive Analysis Hypothesis (CAH) would predict that, where differences exist, errors would be bi-directional, that is, for example, French speakers learning English and English speakers learning French would make errors on parallel linguistic features. To illustrate this, let us examine one way in which French and English differ and how this might be expected to lead to errors.

In English, direct objects, whether nouns or pronouns, come after the verb (for example, 'The dog eats *it*, the dog eats *the cookie*'). In French, direct objects which are nouns follow the verb (for example, 'Le chien mange *le biscuit*'— literally, 'The dog eats the cookie'), but pronoun direct objects precede the verb (for example, 'Le chien *le* mange'—literally, 'The dog it eats'). The CAH would predict that a native speaker of English might say: 'Le chien mange *le*' when learning French, and that a native speaker of French might say 'The dog *it* ate' when learning English.

In fact, research has shown that English speakers learning French are more likely to make the predicted error than French speakers learning English. This may be due to the fact that English speakers learning French hear many examples of sentences with subject–verb–object word order (for example, 'Le chien mange le biscuit'). Thus they make the incorrect assumption—based on both the word order of their first language *and* information from the second language—that all direct objects come after the verb. French-speaking learners of English, on the other hand, hearing and seeing no evidence that English pronoun objects precede verbs, do not tend to make this error. Researchers have also found that learners have intuitions that certain features of their first language are less likely to be transferable than others. For example, most learners believe that idiomatic or metaphorical expressions cannot simply be translated word for word.

As a result of the finding that many aspects of learners' language could not be explained by the CAH, a number of researchers began to take a different approach to analysing learners' errors. This approach, which developed during the 1970s, became known as 'error analysis' and involved a detailed description and analysis of the kinds of errors second language learners make. The goal of this research was to discover what learners really know about the language. As Pit Corder said in a famous article published in 1967, when learners produce 'correct' sentences, they may simply be repeating something they have already heard; when they produce sentences which differ from the target language, we may assume that these sentences reflect the learners' current understanding of the rules and patterns of that language. 'Error analysis' differed from contrastive analysis in that it did not set out to predict errors. Rather, it sought to discover and describe different kinds of errors in an effort to understand how learners process second language data. Error analysis was based on the assumption that, like child language, second language learner language is a system in its own right—one which is rule-governed and predictable.

Larry Selinker gave the name *interlanguage* to learners' developing second language knowledge (Selinker 1972). Analysis of a learner's interlanguage shows that it has some characteristics influenced by the learner's previously learned language(s), some characteristics of the second language, and some characteristics which seem to be very general and tend to occur in all or most interlanguage systems. Interlanguages are systematic, but they are also dynamic, continually evolving as learners receive more input and revise their hypotheses about the second language. In the activity that follows, we will look at some characteristics of interlanguage.

Activity

The Great Toy Robbery

The following texts were written by two learners of English, one a French-speaking secondary school student, the other a Chinese-speaking adult learner. In both cases, the learners saw a cartoon film entitled *The Great Toy Robbery* (National Film Board of Canada). After viewing the film, students were asked to retell the story in writing, as if they were telling it to someone who had not seen the film.

Read the texts and examine the errors made by each learner. Do they make the same kinds of errors? In what ways do the two interlanguages differ?

Learner 1: French first language, secondary school student

> During a sunny day, a cowboy go in the desert with his horse. he has a big hat. His horse eat a flour. In the same time, Santa Clause go in a city to give some surprises. He has a red costume and a red packet of surprises. You have three robbers in the mountain who sees Santa Clause with a king of glaces that it permitted us to see at a long distance. Every robbers have a horse. They go in the way of Santa Clause, not Santa Clause but his pocket of surprises. After they will go in a city and they go in a saloon. [. . .]
>
> (unpublished data from P. M. Lightbown and B. Barkman)

Learner 2: Chinese first language, adult

> This year Christmas comes soon! Santa Claus ride a one horse open sleigh to sent present for children. on the back of his body has big packet. it have a lot of toys. in the way he meet three robbers. They want to take

his big packet. Santa Claus no way and no body help, so only a way give them, then three robbers ride their horse dashing through the town. There have saloon, they go to drink some beer and open the big packent. They plays toys in the Bar. They meet a cow boy in the saloon.

(unpublished data from M. J. Martens)

Many error types are common to both learners. Both make errors of subject–verb agreement (for example, 'a cowboy go' and 'three robbers in the mountain who sees' by learner 1 and 'Santa Claus ride' and 'they plays' by learner 2). Such errors are clearly not due to first language interference. They reflect learners' understanding of the second language system itself rather than an attempt to transfer characteristics of their first language. These are referred to as *developmental errors* because they are errors which might very well be made by children acquiring English as their first language. Sometimes these are errors of *overgeneralization*, that is, errors caused by trying to use a rule in a context where it does not belong, for example, the -s ending on the verb in 'they plays'. Sometimes the errors are better described as *simplification*, where elements of a sentence are left out, for example, or where all verbs have the same form regardless of person, number, or tense.

One can also see, especially in learner 2's text, the influence of classroom experience. An example is the use of formulaic expressions such as 'one horse open sleigh' which is taken verbatim from a well-known Christmas song, which has no doubt been taught and sung in the learner's ESL class. The vivid 'dashing through the town' probably comes from the same source.

For those who are familiar with the English spoken by native speakers of French, some of the errors made by the first learner will readily be recognized as probably based on French. Similarly, those familiar with the English of Chinese speakers may recognize errors made by the Chinese learner as being due to the learner's attempt to use patterns of Chinese in English sentences. These are called *transfer* or 'interference' errors. It is clear, however, that it is very often difficult to determine the source of errors. Thus error analysis has the advantage of permitting a description of some systematic aspects of learner language, but it does not always give us clear insights into what causes learners to do what they do. Furthermore, as Jacquelyne Schachter pointed out in a 1974 article, learners sometimes avoid using certain features of language which they perceive to be difficult for them. This 'avoidance' may lead to the absence of certain errors, but it also leaves the analyst without information about the learners' developing interlanguage. That is, the absence of particular features will be difficult for the researcher or teacher to observe, but this phenomenon of 'avoidance' may also be a part of the learner's systematic second language performance.

Developmental sequences

Research on second language acquisition has revealed that second language learners, like first language learners, pass through sequences of development. Furthermore, in a given language, many of these developmental sequences are similar for first and second language learners. Even among second language learners, these developmental sequences are similar: what is learned early by one is learned early by others, even when they come from different first language backgrounds and different learning environments.

Among first language learners, this is perhaps not so unexpected because their language learning is partly tied to their cognitive development, that is, to their learning about the relationships among people, events, and objects around them. But among second language learners, whose experiences with the language may vary quite widely and whose cognitive development is essentially stable, it is more remarkable that developmental sequences are so similar. Furthermore, although learners obviously need to have opportunities to hear or read certain things before they begin to use them, it is not always the case that those features of the language which are heard most frequently are easiest to learn. For example, virtually every English sentence has one or more articles ('a' or 'the'), but many learners have great difficulty using these forms correctly. Finally, although the learners' first language does have an influence, many aspects of these developmental stages are similar among learners from many different first language backgrounds.

In the next section, the stages of acquisition for specific grammatical features are presented for second language learners. In Chapter 1 we saw some developmental sequences for English child language acquisition of grammatical morphemes, negation, and questions. Researchers in second language acquisition have examined some of these same features, as well as others.

Grammatical morphemes

Several studies to examine the development of grammatical morphemes have been carried out with learners who have learned English as a second language in a natural (non-instructional) environment. These studies were done with learners of different ages and from different first language backgrounds. Like the first language researchers, the second language researchers looked at learners' use of grammatical morphemes such as plural, *-ing*, past tense, etc. They took speech samples from a large number of learners at one point in time and scored each morpheme for accuracy in the learners' speech. This was done by identifying every obligatory context for each morpheme and dividing the number of correctly supplied morphemes by the total number that should have been supplied in a grammatical sentence. The resulting percentage was treated as the accuracy score for this morpheme. These scores were then ranked from highest to lowest, giving an *accuracy order* for the morphemes.

The overall results of the studies suggested an order which, while not the same as the developmental sequence found in the first language studies, was similar among second language learners from different first language backgrounds. For example, most studies showed a higher degree of accuracy for plural than for possessive; for *-ing* than for *-ed* past. This suggests that this accuracy order is not determined entirely by the learners' first language. However, a thorough review of all the 'morpheme acquisition' studies suggests that the learners' first language has a more important influence on acquisition sequences than some researchers would claim. For example, learners whose first language has a possessive *-s* form which resembles the English *'s* (such as German) seem to acquire this form earlier than those whose first language has a very different way of forming the possessive (such as French or Spanish). There are other unanswered questions in the morpheme acquisition literature. For example, some of the similarities and differences observed in different studies seem to be due to the way the language samples were collected. Nevertheless, there are some very strong patterns of similarity which cannot be explained by the influence of the first language alone (see Larsen-Freeman and Long 1991).

Negation

Another example of the interaction between developmental sequences and first language influence is in the acquisition of negation in English. (See Schumann 1979 for a review of research on negation in second language learning.) To a large extent, the acquisition of negative sentences by second language learners follows a path that looks nearly identical to the stages we saw in Chapter 1 for first language acquisition. What is different, however, is that second language learners from different first language backgrounds behave somewhat differently *within* those stages.

Stage 1
The negative element (usually 'no' or 'not') is typically placed before the verb or the element being negated. Often, it occurs as the first word in the utterance because the subject of the sentence is not there.

> No bicycle. No have any sand. I not like it.

'No' is preferred by most learners in this early stage, perhaps because it is the negative form that is easiest to hear and recognize in the speech they are exposed to. Italian and Spanish speakers may prefer 'no' because it corresponds to the negative form in Italian and Spanish.

Stage 2

At this stage, 'no' and 'not' may alternate with 'don't'. However, 'don't' is not marked for person, number, or tense and it may even be used before modals like 'can' and 'should':

> He don't like it. I don't can sing.

Stage 3

Learners begin to place the negative element after auxiliary verbs like 'are', 'is', and 'can'. But at this stage, the 'don't' form is still not fully analysed:

> You can not go there. He was not happy. She don't like rice.

Stage 4

'Do' is marked for tense, person, and number, and most interlanguage sentences appear to be just like those of the target language:

> It doesn't work. We didn't have supper.

For some time, however, learners may continue to mark tense, person, and number on both the auxiliary and the verb:

> I didn't went there. She doesn't wants to go.

This sequence of stages is descriptive of the second language development of most second language learners. However, although it is true that virtually all learners of English seem to pass through a stage of forming negative sentences by placing 'no' before the verb, some learners may stay longer in that stage than others. If a learner's native language forms the negative in just that way (for example, Spanish 'No tienen muchos libros', 'No have many books'), it may take longer for the learner to notice that native speakers of English do *not* form the negative in that way. Similarly, once German speakers reach stage 3 and begin to place the negative marker after the auxiliary, they may also sometimes place it after lexical verbs (for example, German 'Sie kommen nicht nach Hause', 'They come not home').

Questions

Manfred Pienemann and his colleagues have developed a framework for describing second language question stages for learners of English from a variety of first language backgrounds (Pienemann, Johnston, and Brindley 1988). An adapted version of the stages is shown in Table 4.1.

Table 4.1: Developmental stages for question formation (adapted from
Pienemann, Johnston, and Brindley 1988)

Stage 1	**Single words, formulae or sentence fragments**	'Four children?' 'A dog?'
Stage 2	**Declarative word order**	
	no inversion, no fronting:	'It's a monster in the right corner?' 'The boys throw the shoes?'
Stage 3	**Fronting:**	
	wh-fronting, no inversion:	'Where the little children are?' 'What the dog are playing?'
	do-fronting:	'Do you have a shoes on your picture?' 'Does in this picture there is four astronauts?'
	other-fronting:	'Is the picture has two planets on top?'
Stage 4	**Inversion in *wh*- + copula and 'yes/no' questions**	
	wh- + copula:	'Where is the sun?'
	auxiliary other than 'do' in 'yes/no' questions:	'Is there a fish in the water?'
Stage 5	**Inversion in *wh*- questions**	
	inverted *wh*- questions with 'do':	'How do you say [proche]?'
	inverted *wh*- questions with auxiliaries other than 'do':	'What's the boy doing?'
Stage 6	**Complex questions**	
	question tag:	'It's better, isn't it?'
	negative question:	'Why can't you go?'
	embedded question:	'Can you tell me what the date is today?'

It is clear from this figure that second language learners learn to form questions
in a sequence of development which is similar in most respects to first language
question development (see Chapter 1). Even learners whose first language has
subject–auxiliary inversion for questions go through stages of using declarative
word order and a period of 'fronting' in forming questions in English. This
pattern has also been observed in the acquisition of French and German.

The developmental sequence for questions, while very similar across learners,
also appears to be affected by first language influence. For example, even
though German requires subject–verb inversion to form questions ('Können
sie tanzen?', 'Can they dance?'), German learners of English will pass through

a phase of asking questions without inversion. However, once they reach stage 4 and ask English questions with subject–auxiliary inversion, they may assume that subject–verb inversion is also possible. Thus, alongside correct questions such as 'Can I play?' one may hear questions such as 'Play you baseball?'

Activity

Learners' questions

The questions in the chart on page 81 were asked by students in a grade 5 intensive ESL class in Quebec, Canada. The children (aged 10–12) are all French-speaking and have little contact with English outside their English class. In their English classes they spend most of their time in communicative activities, and their teachers rarely correct their errors or focus on specific points of grammar. In many ways, these students have an experience of their second language which is similar to that of learners in an informal language learning setting.

These questions were recorded while the children were playing a picture identification game. Their interlocutor was looking at a picture which was a duplicate of *one* of the four pictures which the students could see. The children asked these questions in order to gather information which would permit them to guess which picture the interlocutor was holding.

Activity

More about questions

Another group of French-speaking learners from the same learning context described in the activity above were asked to judge whether some questions were correct or not. Most of these learners produced stage 2 and 3 questions when they participated in the oral questions game shown above.

The task was a 'preference task' in which learners were presented with pairs of questions and asked to judge whether only one or the other was correct or whether they were both correct or both incorrect. They also had the option of saying 'I don't know.'

Some of the questions the students judged are shown in the chart on page 82. Determine the developmental stage corresponding to each question and whether the question is correct or not. Remember, some stage 3 questions are actually grammatically correct questions. Then, decide which questions you think these learners, who produced mostly stage 2 and 3 questions, were willing to accept and which they rejected.

Based on the information in Table 4.1, can you identify which stage of second language question development each question fits into?

Learner 1   **Stage**
 1 Does a dog is black and white?   1 2 3 4 5 6
 2 Where the dog is?   1 2 3 4 5 6
 3 Does the boy throw a ball?   1 2 3 4 5 6
 4 How many spot the dog has?   1 2 3 4 5 6
 5 It is five questions?   1 2 3 4 5 6

Learner 2
 6 Do you see a dog?   1 2 3 4 5 6
 7 Do the dog has a shoe?   1 2 3 4 5 6
 8 The boy throw a ball or a shoe? 1 2 3 4 5 6
 9 The ball is on the air?   1 2 3 4 5 6
10 The dog has a little spot black? 1 2 3 4 5 6

Learner 3
11 What is the dog doing?   1 2 3 4 5 6
12 Are the children running?   1 2 3 4 5 6
13 Is the shoe on the grass?   1 2 3 4 5 6
14 How many spots does the dog have? 1 2 3 4 5 6
15 Did the dog catch the shoe?   1 2 3 4 5 6

Answer key
Learner 1: Questions 1, 2, and 4 are stage 3: 'does' and 'where' and 'how many' appear simply to be 'fronted' to form a question. Question 5 is stage 2: there has been no adjustment to the word order of a declarative sentence; only the rising intonation identifies the sentence as a question. Question 3 is a bit tricky. It looks like a correct question, but it may be 'correct for the wrong reason'. The evidence from this learner's other questions suggests that 'does' is just the form that is placed in front of a sentence to make a question. That would make Question 3 a stage 3 question, just like Question 1. If the learner had used other forms of 'do' or other auxiliaries to form yes/no questions, it would be a stage 4 question.

Learner 2: Questions 6 and 7 are stage 3: here, 'do' seems to have been placed at the front of the sentence. Questions 8, 9, and 10 are stage 2.

Learner 3: Questions 11 and 14 are stage 5: a *wh-* question with both inversion of the subject and the auxiliary and the second verb ('doing') placed correctly after the subject. Questions 12, 13, and 15 are stage 4: correct subject–verb inversion in 'yes/no' questions. It is clear that these questions are different from the 'does' questions asked by Learner 1 because there are several different auxiliary verbs in the 'yes/no' questions.

Question	Stage 2, 3, 4, 5	Correct/ incorrect	Accepted/ rejected
1 Why do children like McDonald's?			
2 Are you a good student?			
3 Are the students watching TV?			
4 Can I take the dog outside?			
5 Can the children speak Spanish?			
6 What can we watch on TV tonight?			
7 What is your brother doing?			
8 When are you going to eat breakfast?			
9 Do the teachers like to cook?			
10 Do they like pepperoni pizza?			
11 The teachers like to cook?			
12 The children can speak Spanish?			
13 Why fish can live in water?			
14 What your brother is doing?			
15 Why children like McDonald's?			

Answer key

Questions 2, 4, 6, 8, 10 are correct, at stages 4, 4, 5, 5, and 3 respectively. The students overwhelmingly *accepted* these.

Questions 1, 3, 5, 7, 9 are also correct, at stages 5, 4, 5, 5, and 3 respectively. The student overwhelmingly *rejected* these.

Questions 11, 12, 13, 14, and 15 are incorrect questions, at stages 2, 2, 3, 3, and 3 respectively. Students overwhelmingly *accepted* these.

What can the results of this preference task mean? If they produced mostly stage 2 and 3 oral questions, why did students accept some stage 3 questions and reject others? Why did they accept some stage 4 and 5 questions and reject others?

One possible answer to these questions lies in the subject of each sentence. Underline the subject of each question ('children' in question 1; 'you' in question 2, etc.). What do you notice? The correct questions which the students accepted have a pronoun subject (you, I, we, they). The correct questions which they rejected have a noun subject (children, fish, etc.). The incorrect questions which they accepted also have noun subjects.

Further analysis suggests that the students have begun to recognize and even use the rule that requires inversion of the subject and auxiliary verb in English questions. This rule is similar to the rule for question formation in French, their first language. However, they seem to be transferring from French a restriction on this rule. In French, pronoun subjects but not noun subjects can be moved to the post-verbal position. Thus, the French equivalents of the odd numbered questions would *not* be grammatical in French, and the students rejected them in English. The equivalents of the even-numbered questions and questions 11–15 would be considered acceptable in French – although the question formula 'est-ce que' or inversion with an inserted pronoun might also be added to those in questions 11–15.

This aspect of the acquisition of questions is another example of how learners' first language interacts with developmental sequences and is discussed further in Chapter 6.

Relative clauses

A number of studies have found that second language learners first acquire relative clauses which refer to nouns in the subject and direct object positions, and only later (and in some cases, never) learn to use them to modify nouns in other sentence roles (for example, indirect object and object of preposition). A summary of the observed pattern of acquisition for relative clauses is shown in Table 4.2. It is referred to as the 'accessibility hierarchy' and it reflects the apparent ease with which learners have 'access' to certain structures in the target language.

Table 4.2: Accessibility hierarchy for relative clauses in English (adapted from Doughty 1991)

Part of speech	Relative clause
Subject	The girl who was sick went home.
Direct object	The story that I read was long.
Indirect object	The man who[m] I gave the present to was absent.
Object of preposition	I found the book that John was talking about.
Possessive	I know the woman whose father is visiting.
Object of comparison	The person that Susan is taller than is Mary.

Unlike the study of grammatical morphemes, negation, and questions, the study of relative clauses has not been principally inspired by research on child language. The hierarchy was first described in a study of languages of the world. Edward Keenan and Bernard Comrie (1977) found that languages which included the structures at the bottom of his list would also have those at the top, but the opposite was not necessarily true. Research on this aspect of second language development has shown that if a learner can use one of the structures at the bottom of the list, he or she will probably be able to use any that precede it. On the other hand, a learner who can produce sentences with relative clauses in the subject or direct object positions will not necessarily be able to use relatives in any other position.

Reference to past

Another type of developmental sequence has also been described. In this case, the sequence reflects learners' changing ability to express the same meaning. One example of this is the development of reference to past events. Adolescent and adult learners often have important things to say about past events, but their knowledge of the target language limits their ability to do this. A number of researchers, observing learners from different first language backgrounds and acquiring a variety of second languages, have observed a pattern which is similar across learners.

In the beginning, learners with very limited language may simply refer to events in the order in which they occurred or mention a time or place to show that the event occurred in the past.

> My son come. He work in restaurant.
> January. It's very cold.
> Viet Nam. We work too hard.

Later, learners start to attach a grammatical morpheme which shows that the verb is marked for the past.

> The people worked in the fields.

Even after they begin marking past tense on verbs, however, learners may still make errors such as the overgeneralization of the regular *-ed* ending.

> She rided her bicycle.

Another aspect of learning how to refer to the past has been shown in studies by Kathleen Bardovi-Harlig and her colleagues. They found that learners are more likely to mark past tense on some verbs than on others. For example, learners seem to recognize the need to mark past tense more easily in sentences such as 'I broke the vase' and 'My sister fixed it with glue' than in sentences such as 'She seemed happy last week' or 'My father belonged to a club' (Bardovi-Harlig and Reynolds 1995).

Bardovi-Harlig has suggested that these differences are due to the kinds of meanings expressed by the different verbs. Learners seem to find it easier to mark past tense when referring to completed events than when referring to states and activities which may last for extended periods without a clear end-point.

Movement through developmental sequences

We have seen in this section that in second language acquisition there are systematic and predictable stages, or sequences, of acquisition. We have seen examples of this in the development of grammatical morphemes, negatives, questions, relative clauses, and reference to past. It is important to emphasize, however, that developmental stages are not like closed rooms. Learners do not leave one behind when they enter another. In examining a language sample from an individual learner, one should not expect to find all and only examples of behaviours from one stage. On the contrary, at a given point in time, learners may use sentences typical of several different stages. It is perhaps better to think of a stage as being characterized by the emergence and increasing frequency of a particular form rather than by the disappearance of an earlier one. Even when a more advanced stage comes to dominate in a learner's speech, conditions of stress or complexity in a communicative interaction can cause the learner to 'slip back' to an earlier stage.

New ways of looking at first language influence

Researchers rejected the interpretation of contrastive analysis which made 'transfer' or 'interference' the explanation for all of a learner's difficulties with the target language. This was no doubt due in part to the fact that contrastive analysis was closely associated with behaviourist views of language acquisition. In rejecting behaviourism, some researchers also discarded contrastive analysis as a source of valuable information about learners' language.

There is no doubt in the minds of most researchers and teachers, however, that learners draw on their knowledge of other languages as they try to discover the complexities of the new language they are learning. We have seen some ways in which the first language interacts with developmental sequences. When learners reach a certain stage and perceive a similarity to their first language, they may linger longer at that stage (for example, the Spanish speaker's negation) or add a substage (for example, the German speaker's inversion of subject and lexical verbs in questions) to the sequence which, overall, is very similar across learners, regardless of their first language. They may learn a second language rule but restrict its application (for example, the French speaker's rejection of subject–auxiliary inversion with noun subjects).

The first language may influence learners' interlanguage in other ways as well. The phenomenon of 'avoidance' which Jacquelyne Schachter described appeared to be caused at least in part by learners' perception that a feature in the target language was so distant and different from their first language that they preferred not to try it (Schachter 1974)!

Other researchers have also found evidence of learners' sensitivity to degrees of distance or difference and a reluctance to attempt a transfer over too great a distance. In one very revealing study, Håkan Ringbom (1986) found that the 'interference' errors made in English by both Finnish-Swedish and Swedish-Finnish bilinguals were most often traceable to Swedish, not Finnish. The fact that Swedish and English are closely related languages which actually do share many characteristics seems to have led learners to take a chance that a word or a sentence structure that worked in Swedish would have an English equivalent. Finnish, on the other hand, belongs to a completely different language family. This knowledge led learners to avoid using Finnish as a source of possible transfer, whether their own first language was Swedish or Finnish.

The risk-taking associated with this perception of similarity has its limits, however. As we noted earlier, learners seem to know that idiomatic or metaphorical uses of words are often quite unique to a particular language. Eric Kellerman (1986) found that many Dutch learners of English were reluctant to accept certain idiomatic expressions or unusual uses of words such as 'The wave *broke* on the shore' but accepted 'He *broke* the cup' even though both are straightforward translations of sentences with the Dutch verb *breken*.

Another way in which learners' first language can affect second language acquisition is in making it difficult for them to notice that something they are saying is absent from the language as it is used by more proficient speakers. Lydia White (1989) drew attention to the difficulties learners may have when some feature of their interlanguage and their first language are based on patterns which are very similar but not identical. When the learner's interlanguage form does not cause any difficulty in communicating meaning, the learner may find it difficult to get rid of it. Lydia White gives the example of the restrictions on adverb placement in French and English. French and English share considerable flexibility in where adverbs can be placed in simple sentences (see further discussion and references in Chapter 6). However, as the examples in Table 4.3 show, there are some differences. English, but not French, allows SAVO order; French, but not English, allows SVAO.

Second language learners have difficulty in both directions. It seems fairly easy for French-speaking learners of English to notice the new form and to add SVAO to their repertoire and for English-speaking learners of French to add SAVO, but they have far greater difficulty getting rid of the form which does not occur in the target language. English-speaking learners of French make the SAVO error, and French-speaking learners of English make the SVAO error.

Current views of first language influence emphasize that there is an important interaction involving the first language (or other previously learned languages), some universal knowledge or processes, and the samples of the target language which learners encounter in the input. In Chapter 6, we will look at how instruction and metalinguistic information may also contribute to this interaction.

Table 4.3: Adverb placement in French and English

S = Subject   V = Verb   O = Object   A = Adverb
ASVO Often, Mary drinks tea. Souvent, Marie boit du thé.
SVOA Mary drinks tea often. Marie boit du thé souvent.
SAVO Mary often drinks tea. *Marie souvent boit du thé.
SVAO *Mary drinks often tea. Marie boit souvent du thé.
Note: The asterisk (*) means that the sentence is not grammatical.

Summary

The focus in this chapter has been on second language acquisition by people who, although they may receive some instruction, also have considerable exposure to their second language in natural settings—at work, in the schoolyard, in the supermarket, or the neighbourhood laundromat. In general, researchers have found that learners who receive grammar-based instruction still pass through the same developmental sequences and make the same types of errors as those who acquire language in natural settings. For example, in some of the most extensive work on acquisition sequences, Jürgen Meisel and his colleagues Manfred Pienemann and Harald Clahsen found very consistent patterns in the acquisition of German by speakers of several Romance languages who had little or no instruction in German as a second language (Meisel, Clahsen, and Pienemann 1981). Pienemann later found very similar patterns in the acquisition of German word order by speakers of English whose only exposure to the language was in their university German classes in Australia

(Pienemann 1989). In Chapter 6 we will focus on the second language acquisition of learners in classroom settings. First, however, we will look at the classroom itself. In Chapter 5, we will explore the many ways in which researchers have sought to understand the classroom environment for second language acquisition.

Sources and suggestions for further reading

General discussion of learner language

Cook, V. 1991. *Second Language Learning and Language Teaching.* London: Edward Arnold.

Ellis, R. 1997. *Second Language Acquisition.* Oxford: Oxford University Press.

Ellis, R. 1994. *The Study of Second Language Acquisition.* Oxford: Oxford University Press.

Larsen-Freeman, D. and **M. H. Long.** 1991. *An Introduction to Second Language Acquisition.* New York: Longman.

Lightbown, P. M. 1985. 'Great expectations: Second language acquisition research and classroom teaching.' *Applied Linguistics* 6/2: 173–89.

The concept of interlanguage

Corder, S. P. 1967. 'The significance of learners' errors.' *International Review of Applied Linguistics* 5/2–3: 161–9.

Selinker, L. 1972. 'Interlanguage.' *International Review of Applied Linguistics* 10/2: 209–31.

Developmental sequences in second language acquisition

Bardovi-Harlig, K. and **D. Reynolds.** 1995. 'The role of lexical aspect in the acquisition of tense and aspect.' *TESOL Quarterly* 29/1: 107–31.

Meisel, J. M. 1986. 'Reference to past events and actions in the development of natural second language acquisition' in C. Pfaff (ed.): *First and Second Language Acquisition Processes.* Cambridge, Mass.: Newbury House.

Meisel, J. M., H. Clahsen, and **M. Pienemann.** 1981. 'On determining developmental stages in natural second language acquisition.' *Studies in Second Language Acquisition* 3/2: 109–35.

Pienemann, M. 1989. 'Is language teachable? Psycholinguistic experiments and hypotheses.' *Applied Linguistics* 10/1: 52–79.

Pienemann, M., M. Johnston, and **G. Brindley.** 1988. 'Constructing an acquisition-based procedure for second language assessment.' *Studies in Second Language Acquisition* 10/2: 217–43.

Schumann, J. 1979. 'The acquisition of English negation by speakers of Spanish: a review of the literature' in R. W. Andersen (ed.): *The Acquisition and Use of Spanish and English as First and Second Languages.* Washington, D. C.: TESOL. pp. 3–32.

Zobl, H. 1982. 'A direction for contrastive analysis: the comparative study of developmental sequences.' TESOL *Quarterly* 16/2: 169–83.

First language influence

Kellerman, E. 1986. 'An eye for an eye: crosslinguistic constraints on the development of the L2 lexicon.' in E. Kellerman and M. Sharwood Smith (eds.): *Crosslinguistic Influence in Second Language Acquisition.* New York: Pergamon, pp. 35–48.

Odlin, T. 1989. *Language Transfer.* Cambridge: Cambridge University Press.

Ringbom, H. 1986. 'Crosslinguistic influence and the foreign language learning process' in E. Kellerman and M. Sharwood Smith (eds.): *Crosslinguistic Influence in Second Language Acquisition.* New York: Pergamon, pp. 150–72.

Schachter, J. 1974. 'An error in error analysis.' *Language Learning* 24/2: 205–14.

Relative clause hierarchy

Doughty, C. 1991. 'Second language instruction does make a difference.' *Studies in Second Language Acquisition* 13/4: 431–69.

Eckman, F., L. Bell, and **D. Nelson.** 1988. 'On the generalization of relative clause instruction in the acquisition of English as a second language.' *Applied Linguistics* 9/1: 1–20.

Hamilton, R. 1994. 'Is implicational generalization unidirectional and maximal? Evidence from relativization instruction in a second language.' *Language Learning* 44/1: 123–57.

Keenan, E. and **B. Comrie.** 1977. 'Noun phrase accessibility and Universal Grammar.' *Linguistic Inquiry* 8/1: 63–99.

Reference to past

Bardovi-Harlig, K. and **D. Reynolds.** 1995. 'The role of lexical aspect in the acquisition of tense and aspect.' TESOL *Quarterly* 29/1: 107–31.

Meisel, J. M. 1986. 'Reference to past events and actions in the development of natural second language acquisition' in C. Pfaff (ed.): *First and Second Language Acquisition Processes*. Cambridge, Mass.: Newbury House, pp. 206–24.

First language influence

White, L. 1989. *Universal Grammar and Second Language Acquisition*. Amsterdam/Philadelphia, Pa.: John Benjamins.

5 OBSERVING SECOND LANGUAGE TEACHING

In this chapter we will explore different ways in which researchers have observed and described what goes on in second language classrooms. Before we do this, let us take a moment to reflect on the differences between natural and instructional language learning settings. We will then look at transcripts from two classrooms and try to understand what principles guide the teacher in each case.

Comparing instructional and natural settings for language learning

Most people would agree that learning a second language in a natural acquisition context is not the same as learning in the classroom. Many believe that learning on the street is more effective. This belief may be based on the fact that most successful learners have had exposure to the language outside the classroom. What is special about natural language learning? Can we create the same environment in the classroom? Should we? Or are there essential contributions that only instruction and not natural exposure can provide?

Activity

Natural and instructional settings

Natural acquisition contexts should be understood as those in which the learner is exposed to the language at work or in social interaction or, if the learner is a child, in a school situation where most of the other children are native speakers of the target language and where the instruction is directed toward native speakers rather than toward learners of the language.

Traditional instructional environments (for example, grammar translation and audiolingual) are those where the language is being taught to a group of second or foreign language learners. In this case, the focus is on the language itself, rather than on information which is carried by the language. The teacher's goal is to see to it that students learn the vocabulary and grammatical rules of the target language. The goal of learners in such courses is often to pass an examination rather than to use the language for daily communicative interaction.

Communicative, *content-based* and *task-based* instructional environments also involve learners whose goal is learning the language itself, but the style of instruction places the emphasis on interaction, conversation, and language use, rather than on learning *about* the language. The topics which are discussed in communicative and task-based instructional environments are often topics of general interest to the learner, for example, how to reply to a classified advertisement from a newspaper. In content-based instruction, the focus of a lesson is usually on the subject-matter, such as history or mathematics, which students are learning through the medium of the second language. In these classes, the focus may occasionally be on the language itself, but the emphasis is on using the language rather than on talking about it. The language which teachers use for teaching is not selected on the basis of teaching a specific feature of the language, but on leading learners to use the language in a variety of contexts. Students' success in these courses is often measured in terms of their ability to 'get things done' in the second language, rather than on their accuracy in using certain grammatical features.

The chart opposite is similar to the one in Chapter 2 (page 33), in which we compared the profiles of first and second language learners. Think about the characteristics of the different contexts for second language learning. Mark a plus (+) in the chart if the characteristic in the left-hand column is typical of the learning environment in the three remaining columns. Mark a minus (–) if it is not something you usually find in that context. Write '?' if you are not sure.

Characteristics	Natural acquisition	Traditional instruction	Communicative instruction
Error correction			
Learning one thing at a time			
Ample time available for learning			
High ratio of native speakers to learners			
Variety of language and discourse types			
Pressure to speak			
Access to modified input			

Photocopiable © Oxford University Press

As you look at the pattern of + and – signs you have placed in the chart, you will probably find it matches the following descriptions.

When people learn languages at work, in social interactions, or in the playground, their experiences are often quite different from those of learners in classrooms.

In natural acquisition settings

• Learners are rarely corrected. If their interlocutors can understand what they are saying, they do not remark on the correctness of the learners' speech. They would probably feel it was rude to do so.

• Language is not presented step by step. In natural communicative interactions, the learner will be exposed to a wide variety of vocabulary and structures.

• The learner is surrounded by the language for many hours each day. Some of that language is addressed to the learner; much of it is simply 'overheard'.

• The learner usually encounters a number of different people who use the target language proficiently.

- Learners observe or participate in many different types of language events: brief greetings, commercial transactions, exchanges of information, arguments, instructions at school or in the workplace. They may also encounter the written language in the form of notices, newspapers, posters, etc.

- Learners must often use their limited second language ability to respond to questions or get information. In these situations, the emphasis is on getting meaning across clearly, and more proficient speakers tend to be tolerant of errors that do not interfere with meaning.

- Modified input is available in many one-to-one conversations. In situations where many native speakers are involved in the conversation, however, the learner often has difficulty getting access to language he or she can understand.

The events and activities which are typical of traditional instruction differ from those encountered in natural acquisition settings. Traditional classrooms include grammar translation approaches in which there is considerable use of translation activities and grammatical rules, and audiolingual approaches where there is little use of the first language but where learners are expected to learn through repetition and habit formation.

In traditional instructional settings
- Errors are frequently corrected. Accuracy tends to be given priority over meaningful interaction.

- Input is structurally graded, simplified, and sequenced by the teacher and the textbook. Linguistic items are presented and practised in isolation, one item at a time, in a sequence from what is assumed to be 'simple' to that which is 'complex'.

- Learning is often limited to only a few hours a week.

- The teacher is often the only native or proficient speaker the student comes in contact with.

- Students experience a limited range of language discourse types (often a chain of Teacher asks a question/Student answers/Teacher evaluates response). The written language they encounter is selected to represent specific grammatical features rather than for its content.

- Students often feel great pressure to speak or write the second language and to do so correctly from the very beginning.

- Teachers often use the learners' native language to give instructions or in other classroom management events. However, when they use the target language, they tend to modify their language in order to ensure comprehension and compliance.

Not all language classrooms are alike. The conditions for learning differ in terms of the physical environment, the age and motivation of the students, the amount of time available for learning, and many other variables. Classrooms also differ in terms of the principles which guide teachers in their language teaching methods and techniques. Designers of communicative language teaching programs have sought to replace some of the characteristics of traditional instruction with those more typical of natural acquisition contexts. The communicative approach is based on innatist and interactionist theories of language learning and emphasizes the communication of meaning both between teacher and students and among the students themselves in group or pair work. Grammatical forms are focused on only in order to clarify meaning. The assumption is that learners can and must do the grammatical development on their own.

In communicative instructional settings

- There is a limited amount of error correction, and meaning is emphasized over form.

- Input is simplified and made comprehensible by the use of contextual cues, props, and gestures, rather than through *structural grading*.

- Learners usually have only limited time for learning. Sometimes, however, subject-matter courses taught through the second language can add time for language learning. A good example of this is immersion courses where most or all the subject-matter is taught to a group of students who are all second language learners.

- Contact with proficient or native speakers of the language is limited. As with traditional instruction, it is often only the teacher who is a proficient speaker. Learners have considerable exposure to the interlanguage of other learners. This naturally contains errors which would not be heard in an environment where the interlocutors are native speakers.

- A variety of discourse types are introduced through stories, role playing, and the use of 'real-life' materials such as newspapers, television broadcasts, and field trips.

- There is little pressure to perform at high levels of accuracy, and there is often a greater emphasis on comprehension than on production, especially in the early stages of learning.

- Modified input is a defining feature of this approach to instruction. The teacher in these classes makes every effort to speak to students in a level of language they can understand. In addition, other students speak a simplified language.

Activity

Classroom comparisons: teacher–student interactions

In this activity we are going to look at transcripts from two classrooms, one using a structure-based approach to teaching, and the other a communicative approach. Structure-based approaches emphasize language form through either metalinguistic instruction (for example, grammar translation) or pattern practice (for example, audiolingual).

With each transcript, there is a chart for you to check off whether certain things are happening in the interaction, from the point of view of the teacher and of the students. Before you begin reading the transcripts, study the following definitions of the categories used in the grids:

1 *Errors*	Are there errors in the language of either the teacher or the students?
2 *Error feedback*	When errors are made, does the student receive feedback? From whom?
3 *Genuine questions*	Do teachers and students ask questions to which they don't know the answer in advance?
4 *Display questions*	Do teachers ask questions they know the answers to so that learners can display their knowledge of the language (or lack of it)?
5 *Negotiation of meaning*	Do the teachers and students work to understand what the other speakers are saying? What efforts are made by the teacher? By the students?
6 *Metalinguistic comments*	Do the teachers and students talk *about* language, in addition to using it to transmit information?

In the following excerpts, T represents the teacher, S represents a student. (The classroom examples in this chapter come from unpublished data collected by P. M. Lightbown, N. Spada, and B. Barkman.)

Classroom A: A structure-based approach
(Students in this class are 15-year-old French speakers.)

	Teacher	Student
Errors		
Feedback on errors		
Genuine questions		
Display questions		
Negotiation of meaning		
Metalinguistic comments		

T OK, we finished the book—we finished in the book Unit 1, 2, 3. Finished. Workbook 1, 2, 3. So today we're going to start with Unit 4. Don't take your books yet, don't take your books. In 1, 2, 3 we worked in what tense? What tense did we work on? OK?
S Past
T In the past—What auxiliary in the past?
S Did
T Did (writes on board '1–2–3 Past'). Unit 4, Unit 4, we're going to work in the present, present progressive, present continuous—OK? You don't know what it is?
S Yes
T Yes? What is it?
S Little bit
T A little bit
S . . .
T Eh?
S Uh, present continuous
T Present continuous? What's that?
S e–n–g
T i–n–g
S Yes
T What does that mean, present continuous? You don't know? OK, fine. What are you doing, Paul?
S Rien [nothing]
T Nothing?
S Rien—nothing
T You're not doing anything? You're doing *something*!
S Not doing anything.

T You're doing *something*!
S Not doing anything.
T You're doing something—Are, are you listening to me? Are you talking with Marc? What are you doing?
S No, no—uh—listen—uh—
T Eh?
S to you
T You're you're listening to me.
S Yes
T Oh. (writes 'What are you doing? I'm listening to you' on the board)
S Je—
T What are you—? You're excited.
S Yes
T You're playing with your eraser. (writes 'I'm playing with my eraser' on the board). Would you close the door please, Bernard? Claude, what is he doing?
S Close the door
T He is closing the door. (writes 'He's closing the door' on the board) What are you doing, Mario?
S Moi, I listen to you.
T You're listening to me.
S Yes
T OK. Are you sleeping or are you listening to me?
S I don't—moiti—moiti—, half and half.
T Half and half, half sleeping, half listening.

Classroom B: A communicative approach
(Students in this class are 10-year-old French speakers. In this activity, they are telling their teacher and their classmates what 'bugs' them. They have written 'what bugs them' on a card or paper which they hold while speaking.)

	Teacher	Student
Errors		
Feedback on errors		
Genuine questions		
Display questions		
Negotiation of meaning		
Metalinguistic comments		

S It bugs me when a bee string me.
T Oh, when a bee stings me.
S Stings me.
T Do you get stung often? Does that happen often? The bee stinging many times?
S Yeah.
T Often? (Teacher turns to students who aren't paying attention) OK. Sandra and Benoît, you may begin working on a research project, hey? (Teacher turns her attention back to 'What bugs me')
S It bugs me (inaudible) and my sister put on my clothes.
T Ah! She borrows your clothes? When you're older, you may appreciate it because you can switch clothes, maybe. (Turns to check another student's written work) Mélanie, this is yours, I will check.—OK. It's good.
S It bugs me when I'm sick and my brother doesn't help me—my—my brother, 'cause he—me—
T OK. You know—when (inaudible) sick, you're sick at home in bed and you say, oh, to your brother or your sister: 'Would you please get me a drink of water?'—'Ah! Drop dead!' you know, 'Go play in the traffic!' You know, it's not very nice. Martin!
S It bug me to have—
T It bugs me. It bug*zz* me.
S It bugs me when my brother takes my bicycle. Every day.
T Every day? Ah! Doesn't your bro—'(inaudible) his bicycle? Could his brother lend his bicycle? Uh, your brother doesn't have a bicycle?
S Yeah! A new bicycle (inaudible) bicycle.
T Ah, well. Talk to your mom and dad about it. Maybe negotiate a new bicycle for your brother.
S (inaudible)
T He has a new bicycle. But his brother needs a new one too.
S Yes!
T Hey, whoa, just a minute! Jean?
S Martin's brother has—
T Martin, who has a new bicycle? You or your brother?
S My brother.
T And you have an old one.
S (inaudible)
T And your brother takes your old one?
S (inaudible) bicycle
T His bicycle! How old is your brother?
S March 23.
T His birthday?
S Yeah!

T And how old was he?
S Fourteen.
T Fourteen. Well, why don't you tell your brother that when he takes your bike you will take his bike. And he may have more scratches than he figures for. OK?

Characteristics of input in the two classrooms

Classroom A

1 Errors: Very few on the part of the teacher. However the teacher's speech does have some peculiar characteristics typical of this type of teaching, for example, the questions in statement form—often asked with dramatic rising intonation (for example, 'You don't know what it is?'). It's hard to say whether students make errors, because they say as little as possible.

2 Error correction: Yes, whenever students *do* make errors, the teacher reacts.

3 Genuine questions: Yes, a few, but they are almost always related to classroom management. No questions from the students.

4 Display questions: Yes, almost all of the teacher's questions are of this type. Interestingly, however, the students sometimes interpret display questions as genuine questions (T: What are you doing, Paul? S: Rien.). The teacher wants students to produce a sentence—any sentence—in the 'present continuous' but the student worries that he's about to get in trouble for doing 'nothing'.

5 Negotiation of meaning: Very little, learners have no need to paraphrase or request clarifications, and no opportunity to determine the direction of the discourse; the teacher is only focused on the formal aspects of the learners' language. All the effort goes into getting students to produce a sentence with the present continuous form of the verb.

6 Metalinguistic comments: Yes, this is how the teacher begins the lesson and lets the students know what really matters!

Classroom B

1 Errors: Yes, when students speak but hardly ever when the teacher does. Nevertheless, the teacher's speech also contains incomplete sentences, simplified ways of speaking, and an informal speech style.

2 Error correction: Yes, sometimes the teacher repeats what the student has said with the correct form (for example, 'he bug*zz* me'—pointing out the third person singular). However, this correction is not consistent or intrusive as the focus is primarily on letting students express their meanings.

3 Genuine questions: Yes, almost all of the teacher's questions are focused on getting information from the students. The students are not asking questions in this exchange. However, they do sometimes intervene to change the direction of the conversation.

4 Display questions: No, because there is a focus on meaning rather than on accuracy in grammatical form.

5 Negotiation of meaning: Yes, from the teacher's side, especially in the long exchange about who has a bicycle!

6 Metalinguistic comments: No. Even though the teacher clearly hopes to get students to use the third person -*s* in the simple present, she does not say so in these words.

Summary of the two classroom excerpts
You have no doubt noticed how strikingly different these transcripts from the two classrooms are, even though the activities are both teacher-centred. In the transcript from classroom A, the focus is on form (i.e. grammar) and in classroom B, it is on meaning. In classroom A, the only purpose of the interaction is to practise the present continuous. Although the teacher uses real classroom events and some humour to accomplish this, there is no doubt about what really matters here. There is no real interest in what students are doing, but rather in their ability to say it. There is a primary focus on correct grammar, display questions, and error correction in the transcript from classroom A.

In the transcript from classroom B, the primary focus is on meaning, conversational interaction, and genuine questions, although there are some brief references to grammatical accuracy when the teacher feels it is necessary.

Classroom observation schemes

The categories you just used in your examination of the classroom transcripts represent some of the main features which have been used to characterize differences in second language teaching. Many more categories exist and these are often combined to create a *classroom observation scheme*. A classroom observation scheme can be used to describe a range of teacher and learner behaviours. Many different observation schemes have been developed for use in second language classrooms. They differ in several respects including the number of categories they contain, whether they focus on qualitative or quantitative descriptions, whether they are used throughout a lesson or on selected samples of classroom interaction, and whether they are used by observers while they are in the classroom or to analyse audio or video recordings or transcripts of such recordings.

One example of a scheme developed for second language classrooms is the Communicative Orientation of Language Teaching (COLT) Observation Scheme (Spada and Fröhlich 1995). COLT has about 70 categories, which are divided into two parts. Part A describes teaching practices in terms of content, focus, and organization of activity types. Part B describes aspects of the language produced by teachers and students. When using part A, the observer can determine, for example, whether the pedagogical activities are teacher- or learner-centred, whether the focus is on language form or meaning, and whether there are opportunities available for students to choose the topics for discussion. When using part B, the observer can describe, for example, how much (or how little) language students produce, whether their language production is restricted in any way, the kinds of questions teachers ask, and whether and how teachers respond to learners' errors.

The COLT scheme and others like it have been used primarily in classroom research which is intended to examine relationships between differences in teaching practices and differences in second language learning. Observation schemes have also been used in the training of new teachers and in the professional development of experienced ones. The opportunity to observe teaching (including our own) can lead to a greater understanding of the complexities of the teaching process as well as to more critical reflection on our pedagogical practices. Below are some activities that may help you to think about particular aspects of your teaching through self-observation.

Activity

Observing the kinds of questions you ask your students

Most teachers spend a large percentage of classroom time asking questions. As indicated on page 100, questions can be divided into two basic types: display questions and genuine questions. The difference between the two is that display questions are those to which the asker knows the answer in advance, while with genuine questions the answer is not known in advance. Examples of both question types are:

Display question: Are you a student?
                    (asked to a student in a classroom)

Genuine question: Where does your uncle work?
                    (asked to a student when discussing families in class)

Teachers are well known for asking many more display than genuine questions. Indeed, this high frequency of display questions is one of the crucial differences between classroom interaction and conversations in the 'real' world. Researchers have also noted that teachers often give students only a fraction of a second to answer before they move on to another student or answer the question themselves.

Think about the kinds of questions you ask your students. What do you think is the proportion of genuine and display questions that you ask in class? Do you think this varies depending on the activity type? Do you think there is an important role for display questions? If so, in what contexts? To determine the kind of questions you ask in class, complete the following activity.

1 Record a teacher-fronted lesson (not group work).

2 Listen to the tape to see whether you ask more genuine versus display questions.

3 How much time do you allow for students to answer? You may need a stopwatch to answer this question!

4 Are there any differences in the kind of language your students produce when they are asked genuine versus display questions?

Based on your observations do the following:

1 Design an activity which you think will lead to more genuine questions in class. During the activity, try to give students sufficient time to answer.

2 Record this activity.

3 Listen to the recording and focus on the kind of language your students produce when asked genuine questions and given more time to respond.

In addition to (or instead of) recording your own teaching, you might consider observing and recording the class of another teacher.

Feedback in the classroom

As indicated above, several observation schemes have been used in classroom research on second language learning and teaching. Some of them, like COLT, cover a wide range of instructional practices and procedures. Others focus on a specific feature of classroom interaction. For example, Roy Lyster and Leila Ranta developed an instrument which focuses exclusively on descriptions of the different types of feedback on error provided by teachers and the students' immediate responses to them (called *uptake*). This model was developed in French immersion classrooms where second language students learn the target language via subject-matter instruction (i.e. content-based instruction), but it may be used to analyse other types of second language instruction as well.

Lyster and Ranta (1997) developed their model by observing the different types of corrective feedback provided in approximately 20 hours of classroom interaction in four primary French immersion classrooms. They began their observations by using a combination of some categories from part B of the COLT scheme and other categories from models which had examined feedback in both first and second language learning. As they examined the different types of feedback provided in the French immersion classrooms, they adjusted some of the categories to fit their data, and they also developed additional categories. This resulted in the identification of six different feedback types. The definitions below come from the Lyster and Ranta model (1997: 46–8). The examples come from our ESL classroom data.

Explicit correction refers to the explicit provision of the correct form. As the teacher provides the correct form, he or she clearly indicates that what the student had said was incorrect (for example, 'Oh, you mean . . .', 'You should say . . .').

> S The dog run fastly.
> T 'Fastly' doesn't exist. 'Fast' does not take *-ly*. That's why I picked 'quickly'.

Recasts involve the teacher's reformulation of all or part of a student's utterance, minus the error. Recasts are generally implicit in that they are not introduced by 'You mean', 'Use this word', or 'You should say.'

> S1 When you're phone partners, did you talk long time?
> T   When you were phone partners, did you talk for a long time?
> S2 Yes, my first one I talked for 25 minutes
>
> S1 Why you don't like Marc?
> T   Why don't you like Marc?
> S2 I don't know, I don't like him.

Note that in these examples the teacher does not seem to expect uptake from student S1. It seems she is merely repeating the question S1 has asked S2.

Clarification requests indicate to students either that their utterance has been misunderstood by the teacher or that the utterance is ill-formed in some way and that a repetition or a reformulation is required. A clarification request includes phrases such as 'Pardon me . . .' It may also include a repetition of the error as in 'What do you mean by . . . ?'

> T How often do you wash the dishes?
> S Fourteen.
> T Excuse me. (Clarification request)
> S Fourteen.
> T Fourteen what? (Clarification request)
> S Fourteen for a week.
> T Fourteen times a week? (Recast)
> S Yes. Dinner and supper.

Metalinguistic feedback contains comments, information, or questions related to the well-formedness of the student's utterance, without explicitly providing the correct form. Metalinguistic comments generally indicate that there is an error somewhere (for example, 'Can you find your error?'). Also, metalinguistic information generally provides either some grammatical metalanguage that refers to the nature of the error (for example, 'It's masculine') or a word definition in the case of lexical errors. Metalinguistic questions also point to the nature of the error but attempt to elicit the information from the student (for example, 'Is it feminine?').

> S We look at the people yesterday.
> T What's the ending we put on verbs when we talk about the past?

Elicitation refers to at least three techniques that teachers use to directly elicit the correct form from the students. First, teachers elicit completion of their own utterance (for example, 'It's a . . .'). Second, teachers use questions to elicit correct forms (for example, . . . 'How do we say x in French?'). Third, teachers occasionally ask students to reformulate their utterance.

> S My father cleans the plate.
> T Excuse me, he cleans the ???
> S Plates?

Repetition refers to the teacher's repetition, in isolation, of the student's erroneous utterance. In most cases, teachers adjust their intonation so as to highlight the error.

In this example, the repetition is followed by a recast:

> S He's in the bathroom.
> T Bathroom? Bedroom. He's in the bedroom.

Here the repetition is followed by metalinguistic comment and explicit correction:

> S We is . . .
> T We is? But it's two people, right? You see your mistake? You see the error? When it's plural it's we *are*.

In their analysis of the different feedback types, Lyster and Ranta found that all teachers in the content-based French immersion classes they observed used recasts more than any other type of feedback. Indeed, recasts accounted for more than half of the total feedback provided in the four classes. Repetition was the least frequent feedback type provided. The other types of corrective feedback fell in between. Below, the different feedback types are presented in the order of the highest to lowest frequency. Note, however, that some of the feedback types occurred in combination with each other as indicated in some of the examples above.

> Recasts
> Elicitation
> Clarification requests

Metalinguistic feedback
Explicit correction
Repetition.

When Lyster and Ranta examined the students' language behaviour immediately after receiving the different feedback types, they found that student uptake was *least* likely to occur after recasts, and much more likely to occur when they received feedback in the form of elicitations, clarification requests, metalinguistic feedback, and repetitions. Furthermore, elicitations and metalinguistic feedback were more likely to lead to a corrected form of the original utterance.

Lyster has recently argued that students in content-based second language classrooms (where the emphasis is on meaning not form) are less likely to notice recasts than other forms of error correction because when recasts are provided students assume that the teacher is responding to the content rather than the form of their speech (see Lyster 1998). Indeed, the double challenge of making the subject-matter comprehensible and enhancing knowledge of the second language itself within subject-matter instruction has led some to conclude that 'not all content teaching is necessarily good language teaching' (Swain 1988: 68).

In the next chapter, we will examine different views about how languages are best learned in classroom settings and examine some of the research relevant to these positions. This research is directly relevant to questions such as:

1 Is 'comprehensible input' enough for successful second language learning to occur?

2 Is there evidence for the effectiveness of a focus on language form in communicative classrooms?

3 Are some ways of drawing learners' attention to language form more effective than others?

Activity

Analysing classroom interaction

Before we examine these positions and the related research, read the following three transcripts. Look for examples of some of the characteristics of classroom interaction which have been discussed in this chapter.

Overall focus of instruction
Is the instruction in the transcript best described as: ·

Structure-based, where a whole lesson or segment of a lesson is organized around a specific feature of the language and error correction is frequent;

Communication-based, where the lesson focuses primarily on meaning and the communication of messages. Error correction may be provided but it is usually brief and in the midst of an ongoing activity.

Input
What type of input is provided in each transcript? Is it:

Comprehensible input, where meaning is the clear priority in the interaction and no specific aspect of the language seems to be targeted. How would you assess the quality of the comprehensible input in terms of the variety and richness of the language used, the accuracy of the teacher's use of English, the kinds of modifications the teacher makes in making the language comprehensible?
or
Structured input, where the learners' attention is explicitly drawn to a specific feature of language, sometimes with metalinguistic terminology and explanations?

Feedback
In each transcript, what types of corrective feedback types are provided?

Clarification requests, where the teacher indicates to the learner that an utterance has been misunderstood or that there is an error in it and that a repetition or a reformulation is needed;

Recasts, where the teacher repeats a student's utterance, using correct forms where the student has made an error, but does not draw attention to the error and maintains a central focus on meaning;

Elicitations, where the teacher uses questions to elicit completion of students' utterances, asks questions to elicit correct forms, or asks students to reformulate their utterances;

Metalinguistic feedback, where the teacher points to the nature of the error by commenting on or providing information about the well-formedness of a student's utterance (for example, 'Can you see where you made a mistake?'). This can also include metalanguage (for example, 'It's singular not plural').

Transcript 1
French-speaking students in a grade 5 EFL class (ages 10–11) in Quebec are interviewing two older students in grade 7 (ages 12–13), who have come to visit their class. These older students had the same teacher (i.e. Catherine) when they were in grade 5 two years earlier. Students in the class address their questions to the older students individually (i.e. to Beatrice or Mylène) or to both at once.

Some information relevant to the topic of discussion: A typical homework assignment for these classes is to watch a particular television program or to spend a certain amount of time on the phone speaking English with a 'telephone partner' who is another student in the class. Another activity which is referred to is the creation each week of a 'kid of the week' poster, honouring one student in the class. Each student and the teacher write something funny or complimentary about the chosen student on a poster which shows drawings or photos of the student.

(T represents the teacher and S represents a grade 5 student. For the two visiting grade 7 students, M represents Mylène and B, Beatrice.)

S When you're older, do you want kids?
M No.
T Why not? You say that like you're sure. Why not?
M We want no troubles.
T I agree. What about you Beatrice?
B Two, I want two.
T You want two kids?
B If I can, I want one and one.
T That would be nice if you can order what you want. I'll take one girl all-dressed and one boy toasted. That would be nice if you could order them, right, in a restaurant. I want my girl ten years old and the boy 12 years old. No babies. Alright, interesting question Marianne. Geneviève.
S For the both.
T Both of them.
S Were you the phone partner before?
T For one week eh? They were phone partners. Beatrice.
S Beatrice. When you get—
T When you got—it's past.
S When you got the poster did you um . . . ?
T Did you get it the same time? Like the same week?
B No.
T No, I don't think so eh? Yves.
S Mylène, did you watch Cosby show?
T Here you mean?
M Yes.
T Do you watch it sometime? In front of the TV? And then the family watches too. All right.
S What did you like the best?
M Kate and Alley.
T You preferred Kate and Alley? Interesting. But it's not on now. Marc.
S Who's have uh, the—
T Who was the first to get the kid of the week poster?
B I was.
T You were the first one in group? Ah ha. Annie-Claude. Phil?

S   When you're phone partners, did you talk long time?

T   When you were phone partners, did you talk for a long time?

M   Yes. My first one I talked for 25 minutes.

T   The very first one you did eh? I remember that. I said to the kids five minutes for phone conversations and the first time—who was your partner? Do you remember who your partner was?

M   Marie-France.

T   Marie-France. Oh boy. She was funny. Oh God what a clown that girl was. Remember her doll show and tell? She was so funny. We were laughing so much I was crying. Her first phone partner homework she talked for 45 minutes, first time. Annick.

S   When you are in—

T   When you were—

S   Were in this program (?)

B   No, it was Kate and Alley.

T   We had a different show to watch. Kate and Alley. But Kate and Alley is not on now, so that's why we watch Cosby. OK. *Is* and the past is (writing on board)

S   *was*

T   *was. Are*, the past is . . . ?

S   *were*

T   *were. Were* you, not *are* you. Not, I *am, am* I it's *was* I. Caroline.

Transcript 2

This was also recorded in a grade 5 class (age 10). The students and teacher are discussing the 'telephone partners' homework.

T   Telephone partners. Vincent and Victoria did you talk on the phone last night? Yes? Charlie and Nathalie . . . well Charlie and Nathalie . . . Yes? Éric and Christian?

S   Yes.

T   You're going to lose your chair if you continue . . . all right . . . OK. Next . . . what do you have to report about telephone partners? Do you have new partners? Anything interesting happen?

S   Yes, I talk 15 minutes with Christian . . . super funny at the phone.

T   Who's super funny you or Christian?

S   Her . . . n . . . him . . .

T   Yea?

S   . . . her.

T   Yea? Does he tell jokes?

S   Yes (2 voices) . . . Row . . . row . . .

S   What? I don't understand.

T   Oh well, that's Christian. All right, Victoria?

S   (inaudible)

T   OK . . . Yes?

S   (inaudible) . . . 35 minutes.

T   35?

S   Yes . . . about . . . and . . .

T   Does he talk a lot on the phone?

S   Yes.

T   He talks more on the phone than in class?

S   Ah . . . yes.

T   Oh, good. All right, Mark?

S   (inaudible) . . . partner . . . we were talking about . . . there on the phone.

T   They were on the phone the same time as you?

S   Yes.

T   Talking to you?

S   . . . thing . . . same line . . .

T   In English or French?

S   No sometimes in French but ah, in French . . . in ah, and the other one . . . in English.

T   So you just say, 'If you're going to insult me, insult me in English at least eh?'

S   And Mark . . . Mark he . . . ah, Annie, Annie . . . he ah

T   Eh?

S   And Mark . . . he . . . ah, Annie, Annie . . . he ah

T   Annie, that's your sister?

S   Yes and . . . Mark, he was yelling . . . on the phone . . . and . . . back and he was yelling.

T   Mark was yelling?

S   Yes.

T   Quiet. Mark yelled? Ahh! We know a secret? OK, interesting, Annie?

S   I talked to Eric. I talked 15 minutes, I think he . . . I think he . . . with Mark . . . just like Matthew . . .

T   He talked like Matthew?

S   No, just like Matthew his partner . . .

Transcript 3

This was recorded in a class of grade 10 students (age 15) who had been taking English as a second/foreign language classes for a few hours a week since grade 5 (age 10). The activity involves students beginning to work on a homework assignment. The teacher works either with individuals or with the whole group.

T   Keep that and pass it on . . . (handing out homework sheets). Come on!

S   (mutters and coughs)

T   Shh! Which tense is that?

S   Present?

T   What do you change present to?
S   Ah!
T   What tense is that? What tense is that? You finished? You can start your homework.
S   (no response)
T   Mary is a he? Ah ah . . . What tense is that? What do we change past to? What's the past perfect of the verb have? Mary did you do your homework?
S   (no response)
S   Can we write uh . . . the same?
T   No, no, you can write it on the sheet. It's not necessary to, it's not necessary, you can just write it on that . . . save uh save your money . . . How many people are not finished with the blackboard? OK, Go on.
S   (Several students raise their hands)
T   Which tense is that?
S   Uh . . . uh . . . present?
T   What tense is that?
S   (no response)
T   Something wrong?
S   Yes.
T   I think you'd better take another look. How you doing? Ah, past, must change to, always look back if you're not sure.
S   Past.
T   Which one? This one? Yeah?
S   (no response)
T   This is past . . . simple past. OK. Who is talking?
S   (no response)
T   Right. OK. So, wait. (sighs) Stéphane! Stéphane! Stéphane! What verb is that?
S   Can you tell me. Excuse me?
T   What verb is it? Just tell me the name of the verb.
S   Have?
T   Have. What verb is that?
S   Know.
T   Which is which verb?
S   Yeah, I know . . . too . . . because, you change past, for past perfect.
T   Right.
S   Oh . . .
T   But why did you put,
S   Have had a party?
T   Yes!
S   Hein?
S   Had had . . .

S Had /aed/ had . . .

T Uh, you got a problem. Ooh? what's the past participle of go?

S (group grumbles)

S Have gone.

T Shh! How many people are still not finished with the blackboard exercise?

S (some raise hands)

T OK . . . couple of more minutes. When you're finished, do the sentences on the sheet. If you don't finish it in the class, you have to finish for homework. So I suggest you start working. Write, yeah numbers one to twenty.

S Can we answer on the same sheet?

T Yes. You can use the sheet. You don't have to use the piece of paper.

S (muttering)

T Said to . . . said to . . . when we have said to what do we change it to?

S Aha!

T OK, for each sentence to . . . what's your problem? We couldn't. N apostrophe T. Guy?

S (Guy stops doing whatever it was)

T Thank you.

S (group laughs)

T No, the possessive, your . . . right? I have my pencil? You have your pencil? We have . . .

S Your?

T Not your. It's either said to me or tells me not tells to.

S Uh . . .

T And what tense is that . . . said?

S Past?

T Yeh . . . everybody . . . E V E R Y . . .

S Oh.

T OK? Is there anyone who's still not finished with the blackboard?

S Luc . . .

S (group laughs)

T Really?

S Yep.

T Well, if you'd stop talking.

S (class laughs)

T What tense is that? What do you change it to?

S What tense is that?

T Past tense of the verb do. No, I *did* my work. She *did*. QUESTIONS?

S Oh . . .

T It's not necessary to use a sheet of paper. You know. Yes, you can do it on the sheet. Save yourself some money, it's not necessary to . . .

S   (inaudible)
T   Boy, you're really zipping along there, aren't you Guy?
S   Ha ha.

Summary of transcripts

The three transcripts differ in several ways. The first two transcripts represent lessons which have meaning as their primary focus and the third transcript is a lesson in which form is emphasized. However, the first two transcripts also differ from one another in important ways. Below is a summary description of the three transcripts with reference to the specific features outlined on pages 106–7.

The segment of the lesson presented in Transcript 1 represents instruction which is best described as communication-based. The emphasis in this activity is on communicating messages where meaning is the clear priority in the interaction. Thus, the type of input provided is comprehensible input. This does not mean that there is no corrective feedback. On the contrary, the teacher often interrupts briefly to provide students with feedback on their errors. As seen in the transcript, the teacher's corrective feedback also varies. She uses recasts several times and also clarification requests, elicitations, and metalinguistic feedback. None of these corrective strategies interferes with the overall focus on meaning and communication.

Transcript 2 represents a lesson in which there is an exclusive focus on meaning. No particular aspect of language is targeted and there is virtually no corrective feedback provided. When the teacher does provide correction, it is almost always in response to the content and not the form of a student's utterance. Thus, this segment represents a communication-based lesson but differs quite considerably from Transcript 1 in that there is no attention to language form. The type of input provided is comprehensible input.

Transcript 3 differs significantly from Transcripts 1 and 2. In this lesson the emphasis is on a particular grammatical form and there is considerable metalinguistic instruction. Thus, this segment is best described as structure-based and there is a considerable amount of structured input. The teacher's corrective feedback is also primarily metalinguistic with very few recasts or elicitations.

Activity

Observing how you respond to students' errors

Even experienced teachers may discover differences between what they *think* they do and what they *actually* do in their classrooms, and the experience of observing themselves (on video) or examining their language behaviour (via audio-recordings) can be quite revealing. For example, some teachers report that they never (or rarely) correct students' errors. After observing themselves, however, they discover that they do give feedback on error but in ways which are different than they had expected. For example, a teacher may never provide metalinguistic explanations when students make errors but may instead react with a variety of facial expressions, gestures, or shifts in intonation. In this activity, focus on your error-correction behaviour by following the instructions below.

In a class you are teaching:

1 Choose an activity which is teacher-centred but where students have opportunities to speak frequently.

2 Video or audio-record 20 minutes of this activity.

3 Listen to the recording. Focus your attention on whether you provide learners with feedback on the forms they use to express themselves. How often do you do this?

4 Are there particular errors that you always (or almost always) correct? Are there others that you do not correct—either because you chose not to correct or because you did not notice them at the time?

5 Do you have a tendency to react to different errors in different ways (for example, do you respond to vocabulary errors more often or in ways that differ from the frequency and type of correction you give when grammatical errors are made)?

6 How do you draw learners' attention to their errors? Do you provide the corrrect form, for example through recasts? Or do you create an opportunity for students to self-correct, for example, through elicitation, requests for clarification, or simply by a gesture or facial expression that draws their attention to a problem? Do you vary your error-correction procedures or do you tend to use the same procedure all the time?

After this self-observation and analysis, think about what you have learned about your approach to error correction. Were there any surprises? Did you discover an error-correction strategy that you were unaware of using? Perhaps you discovered a particular strategy that seemed to be more effective than another. If so, you might consider doing the follow-up activity described below.

1 Video or audio-record another lesson.

2 Use only one error-correction strategy in this lesson (or a portion of it).

3 In another lesson (or portion of it), use a different error-correction strategy and record this as well.

(Note: Use a similar activity for both error-correction strategies).

4 Watch or listen to the tapes to see if there are any differences in the students' responses to the different types of error correction. You will probably need to do this several times.

In addition to (or instead of) recording your own teaching, you might consider observing and recording the class of another teacher.

Summary

In this chapter we have described some of the ways in which different features of second language instruction can be characterized. We have presented descriptions and examples of how classrooms differ in terms of their overall instructional focus, and the type of input and corrective feedback, and you have had an opportunity to observe your own teaching behaviour. In Chapter 6 we will examine some of the classroom research which has investigated relationships between second language learning and different types of instructional input, interaction, and corrective feedback.

Sources and suggestions for further reading

Classroom observation schemes

Allwright, R. L. 1988. *Observation in the Language Classroom.* London: Longman.

Chaudron, C. 1988. *Second Language Classrooms: Research on Teaching and Learning.* Cambridge: Cambridge University Press.

Long, M. 1980. 'Inside the "black box": Methodological issues in classroom research on language learning.' *Language Learning* 30/1: 1–42.

Malamah-Thomas, A. 1987. *Classroom Interaction.* Oxford: Oxford University Press.

Spada, N. and **M. Fröhlich.** 1995. *The Communicative Orientation of Language Teaching Observation Scheme: Coding Conventions and Applications.* Sydney: National Centre for English Language Teaching and Research, Macquarie University.

Wajnryb, R. 1992. *Classroom Observation Tasks: A Resource Book for Language Teachers and Trainers.* Cambridge: Cambridge University Press.

Corrective feedback models

Lyster, R. 1998. 'Recasts, repetition and ambiguity in L2 classroom discourse.' *Studies in Second Language Acquisition* 20/1: 51–81.

Lyster, R. and **L. Ranta.** 1997. 'Corrective feedback and learner uptake: Negotiation of form in communicative classrooms.' *Studies in Second Language Acquisition* 19/1: 37–61.

Language and content teaching

Swain, M. 1988. 'Manipulating and complementing content teaching to maximize second language learning.' TESL *Canada Journal* 6/1: 68–83.

6 SECOND LANGUAGE LEARNING IN THE CLASSROOM

Five proposals for classroom teaching

The teaching methodologies in the classroom transcripts which were presented in Chapter 5 differ because they reflect different theoretical views concerning the most effective way to learn a second language in classroom settings.

Theories have been proposed for the best way to learn a second language in the classroom and teaching methods have been developed to implement them. But the only way to answer the question 'Which theoretical proposal holds the greatest promise for improving language learning in classrooms settings?' is through research which specifically investigates relationships between teaching and learning.

Both formal and informal research are needed. Formal research involves careful control of the factors which may affect learning. It often uses large numbers of teachers and learners in order to try to limit the possibility that the unusual behaviour of one or two individuals might create a misleading impression about what one would expect in general. Researchers doing this kind of work must sometimes sacrifice naturalness in order to ensure that only those factors under investigation are different in the groups being compared.

Informal research often involves small numbers, perhaps only one class with one teacher, and the emphasis is not on what is most general but rather on what is particular about this group or this teacher. While formal research may add strength to theoretical proposals, informal research, including that carried out by teachers in their own classrooms, is also essential. It is hardly necessary to tell experienced teachers that what 'works' in one context may fail in another.

In this chapter, we examine five proposals for classroom teaching, provide examples from classroom interaction to illustrate how the proposals get translated into classroom practice, and discuss how the findings from some of the formal research in SLA fit them. For each proposal, a few relevant studies will be presented, discussed, and compared with one another. The labels we have given these proposals are:

1 Get it right from the beginning
2 Say what you mean and mean what you say
3 Just listen . . . and read
4 Teach what is teachable
5 Get it right in the end

1 Get it right from the beginning

The 'Get it right from the beginning' proposal for second language teaching probably best describes the way in which many of us were taught a second language in school. It includes the traditional approaches discussed in Chapter 5—grammar translation and audiolingual approaches.

The examples below reflect audiolingual language teaching. The emphasis is on the oral language, but students rarely use the language spontaneously. Teachers avoid letting beginning learners speak freely because this would allow them to make errors. The errors, it is said, could become habits. So it is better to prevent these bad habits before they happen.

Example 1
(A group of 15-year-old students involved in an exercise based on the simple present of English verbs.)

> S1 And uh, in the afternoon, uh, I come home and uh, uh, I uh, washing my dog.
> T   I wash.
> S1 My dog.
> T   Every day you wash your dog?
> S1 No. [ben]
> S2 Il n'a pas de chien! (= He doesn't have a dog!)
> S1 Non, mais on peut le dire! (= No, but we can say we do!)

Clearly, in this case, the student's real experience with his dog (or even the fact that he did or did not have a dog) was irrelevant. What mattered was the correct use of the simple present verb!

Example 2
(A group of 12-year-old learners of English as a foreign language.)

> T   Repeat after me. Is there any butter in the refrigerator?
> Class Is there any butter in the refrigerator?
> T   There's very little, Mom.
> Class There's very little, Mom.

T	Are there any tomatoes in the refrigerator?
Class	Are there any tomatoes in the refrigerator?
T	There are very few, Mom.
Class	There are very few, Mom. (etc.)

Pure repetition. The students have no reason to get involved or to think about what they are saying. Indeed, some students who have no idea what the sentences mean will successfully repeat them anyway, while their minds wander off to other things.

Research findings

Many adult learners, especially those with good metalinguistic knowledge of their own language, express a preference for structure-based approaches. Audiolingual approaches were used successfully with highly motivated adult learners in training programs for government personnel in the United States. However, there is little classroom research to support such approaches for students in ordinary school programs. In fact, it was the frequent failure of traditional grammar translation and audiolingual methods to produce fluency and accuracy in second language learners which led to the development of more communicative approaches to teaching in the first place.

Supporters of communicative language teaching have argued that language is not learned by the gradual accumulation of one item after another. They suggest that errors are a natural and valuable part of the language learning process. Furthermore, they believe that the motivation of learners is often stifled by an insistence on correctness in the earliest stages of second language learning. These opponents of the 'Get it right from the beginning' proposal argue that it is better to encourage learners to develop 'fluency' before 'accuracy'.

Recently, some researchers and educators have reacted to the trend toward communicative language teaching and have revived the concern that allowing learners too much 'freedom' without correction and explicit instruction will lead to early *fossilization* of errors. Once again we hear the call for making sure that learners 'get it right from the beginning'.

Unfortunately, little research has been done to test the hypothesis that a primary emphasis on form in the early stages of second language learning will, in the long run, lead to higher levels of linguistic performance and knowledge than that which is achieved when the primary emphasis is on meaning in the early stages. In order to do such research, it is necessary to compare groups which are similar in all respects except for the type of instruction they receive. However, it is not easy for researchers to find proper comparison groups. On the one hand, there are many parts of the world where one finds only traditional types of language teaching, with their emphasis on learning metalinguistic information and performing accurately from the beginning. In these settings, there are no classrooms where the teaching places the primary emphasis on meaning in the early stages of learning. On the other hand, the widespread adoption of communicative language teaching in recent years has meant that, in other parts of the world, it is very difficult to make comparisons with classrooms which are primarily form-oriented because such classes simply do not exist. Nonetheless, some findings from second language classroom research do permit us to assess the effect of instruction which is strongly oriented to the 'Get it right from the beginning' approach. These include descriptive studies of the interlanguage development of second language learners in audiolingual programs (study 1), and studies of the development of second language proficiency in classroom learners who have received different amounts of form- and meaning-based instruction (studies 2 and 3).

Study 1: Audiolingual pattern drill

In the late 1970s, Patsy Lightbown and her colleagues in Quebec, Canada, carried out a series of longitudinal and cross-sectional investigations into the effect of audiolingual instruction on the second language interlanguage development of francophone ESL learners, aged 11–16 (Lightbown 1983, 1987). Students in these programs typically participated in the types of rote repetition and *pattern practice drill* we saw in examples 1 and 2.

The researchers compared aspects of the learners' acquisition of English grammatical morphemes (such as plural -*s* and the progressive -*ing*) with the 'natural' order of acquisition by uninstructed second language learners. The results indicated several differences between the 'natural order' and the order in which these classroom learners produced them. These findings suggested that the type of instruction provided, a regular diet of isolated pattern practice drills, contributed to the alterations in the learners' natural interlanguage development. However, while learners were able to produce a particular form (i.e. the -*ing* form) with a high degree of accuracy for a time after their instruction had focused on it, the same form was produced with considerably less accuracy (and frequency) when it was no longer being practised in class and when another form (i.e. third person singular simple present) was being drilled instead. These findings provided evidence that an almost exclusive focus on accuracy and practice of particular grammatical forms does not mean that learners will be able to use the forms correctly outside the classroom drill setting or to continue to use them correctly once other forms are introduced. Not surprisingly, this type of instruction did not seem to favour the development of fluency and communicative abilities either.

Study 2: Grammar plus communicative practice

Sandra Savignon (1972) studied the linguistic and communicative skills of 48 college students enrolled in French language courses at an American university.

The students were divided into three groups, all of which received the same number of hours per week of audiolingual instruction where the focus was on the practice and manipulation of grammatical forms. However, the 'communicative group' had an additional hour per week devoted to communicative tasks in an effort to encourage practice in using French in meaningful, creative, and spontaneous ways; the 'cultural group' had an additional hour devoted to activities, conducted in English, which were designed to 'foster an awareness of the French language and culture through films, music, and art'; and the *control group* had an additional hour in the language laboratory doing grammar and pronunciation drills similar to those which they did in their regular class periods.

Tests to measure learners' linguistic and communicative abilities were administered before and after instruction to see if there were any significant differences between groups on these measures. The tests of 'linguistic competence' included a variety of grammar tests, teachers' evaluations of speaking skills, and course grades. The tests of *communicative competence* included measures of fluency and of the ability to understand and transmit information in a variety of tasks, which included: (1) discussion with a native speaker of French, (2) interviewing a native speaker of French, (3) the reporting of facts about oneself or one's recent activities, and (4) a description of ongoing activities.

The results revealed no *significant differences* between groups on the linguistic competence measures. However, the 'communicative group' scored significantly higher than the other two groups on the four communicative tests developed for the study. Savignon interprets these results as support for the argument that second language programs which focus *only* on accuracy and form do not give students sufficient opportunity to develop communication abilities in a second language.

Study 3: Grammar plus communicative practice
In a similar study, Carol Montgomery and Miriam Eisenstein (1985) followed a group of adult learners receiving an additional communicative component to their regular, grammar-based instruction. This group was compared to one which received only the grammar course. The researchers reported that beginner and intermediate-level ESL learners engaging in communicative activities in addition to their regular, required grammar course made greater improvements in accent, vocabulary, grammar, and comprehension than did learners who received only the required grammar course. Somewhat unexpectedly, the area of greatest improvement for the group getting 'real world' communicative practice was in grammatical accuracy.

Interpreting the research
The studies reviewed above provide evidence to support the intuitions of teachers and learners that instruction based on the 'Get it right from the

beginning' proposal has important limitations. Learners receiving audio-lingual or grammar-based instruction are often unable to communicate their messages and intentions effectively in a second language. Experience has also shown that primarily or exclusively grammar-based approaches to teaching do *not* guarantee that learners develop high levels of accuracy and linguistic knowledge. In fact, it is often very difficult to determine what such learners know about the target language; the classroom emphasis on accuracy usually results in learners who are inhibited and will not 'take chances' in using their knowledge for communication. The results from these studies support the claim that learners benefit from opportunities for communicative practice in contexts where the emphasis is on understanding and expressing meaning.

It is important to emphasize that in the Savignon and the Montgomery and Eisenstein studies, all subjects received their regular, grammar-focused instruction and differed only in terms of the presence or absence of an additional communicative practice component. In other words, these studies offer support for the hypothesis that meaning-based instruction is advantageous, *not* that form-based instruction is not. The contributions of communicative practice and grammar-focused instruction will be discussed in more detail in relation to the 'Teach what is teachable' and 'Get it right in the end' proposals.

2 Say what you mean and mean what you say

This is the theoretical view underlying the teacher–student behaviour in the transcript from classroom B (in Chapter 5). Based on the interactionists' hypothesis, advocates of 'Say what you mean and mean what you say' emphasize the necessity for learners to have access to meaningful and comprehensible input through conversational interactions with teachers and other students. They argue that when learners are given the opportunity to engage in meaningful activities, they are compelled to 'negotiate for meaning', that is, to express and clarify their intentions, thoughts, opinions, etc., in a way which permits them to arrive at a mutual understanding. This is especially true when the learners are working together to accomplish a particular goal, for example in task-based instruction. The negotiation, in turn, they claim, leads learners to acquire the language forms—the words and the grammatical structures—which carry the meaning they are attending to.

Negotiation for meaning is accomplished through a variety of modifications which naturally arise in interaction. For example, learners will ask each other or their teacher for clarification, confirmation, repetition, and other kinds of information as they attempt to negotiate meaning. This can be seen in the transcripts from classroom B.

Look for cases of negotiation for meaning in the examples below and compare this with the examples given for the 'Get it right from the beginning' proposal.

Example 3
(The teacher and students from classroom B (pages 98–100). Students are checking answers on a written task.)

    S Me and Josée, we don't have the same as her.
    T That's fine. Yeah, because there'll be different answers.
    S Why . . . uh, we do that with a partner?
    T Simply so you can consult.

(In examples 4, 5, and 6, a group of 12-year-old students are discussing with their teacher a questionnaire about their pets.)

Example 4

    S The fish is difficult to wash?
    T Fish is difficult to wash?
    S Yes.
    T Fish . . . Oh, not so difficult. Fish are difficult to wash?!? What's your uh . . . [question]?
    S Do you have an animal? Yes, I do. Do you ever feed it? Yes, r—
    T Do you know what 'feed' means?
    S Ah, no. It's uh . . .?
    T To give food to it.

Example 5

    T How often do you walk your dog?
    S Never.
    T Why?
    S Because I don't have a dog.

Example 6

    S And what is 'feed'?
    T Feed? To feed the dog?
    S Yes, but when I don't have a . . .
    T If you don't have a dog, you skip the question.

Example 7
(Students from classroom B, doing a morning warm-up activity.)

    T   How are you doing this morning?
    S1 I'm mad!
    S2 Why?
    T   Oh boy. Yeah, why?
    S1 Because this morning, my father say no have job this morning.
    T   Your father has no more job this morning? Or you have no job?
    S1 My father.

How different these examples are from the essentially meaningless interaction often observed in classrooms where the emphasis is on 'getting it right from the beginning'. Such genuine exchanges of information must surely enhance students' motivation to participate in language learning activities. But do they, as advocates of this position claim, lead to successful language acquisition?

Research findings

Most of the research which has directly examined the 'Say what you mean and mean what you say' proposal has been descriptive in nature, focusing on such issues as: How does negotiation which takes place in classrooms differ from that observed in natural settings? How does teacher- versus student-centred classroom organization contribute to differences in conversational interaction? Do task types contribute to different kinds of interactional modifications? Several studies have also examined relationships between modifications in conversational interaction and comprehension. Some recent research has taken the next step and explored the effects of interaction on the acquisition of specific linguistic features. Here are a few studies relevant to the interactionist proposal.

Study 4: Group work and learner language

One of the earliest studies to measure the different types of interaction patterns in second language settings was carried out by Michael Long and his colleagues (1976). In their study with adult learners of English as a foreign language in Mexico, differences in the quantity and quality of student language in group-work versus teacher-centred activities were investigated. They found that the students produced not only a greater quantity but also a greater variety of speech in group work than in teacher-centred activities. Not surprisingly, in the teacher-centred activities, the students primarily responded to the teacher's questions and rarely initiated speech on their own. In contrast, learner language in group-work activity was filled with questions and responses and many more occasions where learners took the initiative to speak spontaneously. In addition, the learner-centred activities led to a much greater variety of language functions (for example, disagreeing, hypothesizing, requesting, clarifying, and defining).

Although this study was small, involving only two pairs of learners and two 40-minute lessons, it was one of the first studies to suggest how opportunities for more group-work interaction may be beneficial for second language learning.

Study 5: Learners talking to learners

Patricia Porter examined the language produced by adult learners performing a task in pairs. There were 18 subjects in the study: 12 non-native speakers of English whose first language was Spanish, and 6 native English speakers. The non-native speakers were intermediate or advanced learners of English.

Each subject was asked to participate in separate discussions with a speaker from each of the three levels. For example, an intermediate-level speaker had a conversation with another intermediate-level speaker, with an advanced-level speaker, and with a native speaker of English. The investigator wanted to compare the speech of native and non-native speakers in conversations as well as to compare differences across proficiency levels in these conversation pairs.

Learners talked more with other learners than they did with native speakers. Also, learners produced more talk with advanced-level than with intermediate-level partners, partly because the conversations with advanced learners lasted longer. Porter examined the number of grammatical and vocabulary errors and false starts and found that learner speech showed no differences across contexts. That is, intermediate-level learners did not make any more errors with another intermediate-level speaker than they did with an advanced or native speaker. This is a particularly interesting finding because it calls into question the argument that learners need to be exposed to a native-speaking model (i.e. teacher) at all times if we are to ensure that they produce fewer errors.

Overall, Porter concluded that although learners cannot always provide each other with the accurate grammatical input, learners can offer each other genuine communicative practice which includes negotiation of meaning. Supporters of the 'Say what you mean and mean what you say' proposal argue that it is precisely this negotiation of meaning which is essential for language acquisition. (See Long and Porter 1985 for further discussion.)

Study 6: Learner language and proficiency level
George Yule and Doris Macdonald (1990) investigated whether the role that different-level learners play in a two-way communication tasks led to differences in their interactive behaviour. In order to do this they set up a task which required two learners to communicate information about the location of different buildings on a map and the route to get there. One learner, referred to as the 'sender', had a map with a delivery route on it, and this speaker's job was to describe the delivery route to the other learner so that he or she could draw the delivery route on a similar map. The task was made more challenging by the fact that there were minor differences between the two maps.

To determine whether there would be any difference in the nature of the interactions according to the relative proficiency of the 40 adult participants, different types of learners were paired together: one group which consisted of high-proficiency learners in the 'sender' role and low-proficiency learners in the 'receiver' role, and another group with low-proficiency 'senders' paired with high-proficiency 'receivers'.

The results showed that when low-proficiency learners were in the 'sender' role, the interactions were considerably longer and more varied than when high-proficiency learners were the 'senders'. The explanation provided for this was that high-proficiency 'senders' tended to act as if the lower-level 'receiver' had very little contribution to make in the completion of the task. As a result, the lower-level 'receivers' were almost forced to play a very passive role and said very little in order to complete the task. When lower-level learners were in the 'sender' role, however, much more negotiation of meaning and a greater variety of interactions between the two speakers took place. Based on these findings, the researchers argue that teachers should sometimes place more advanced students in less dominant roles in paired activities with lower-level learners.

Study 7: Interaction and comprehensibility

In one of the studies to investigate effects of different input conditions on comprehension, Teresa Pica, Richard Young, and Catherine Doughty (1987) found that modified interaction led to higher levels of comprehension than modified input. In their study, 16 adult learners were asked to follow instructions and complete a task under one of two different conditions. In the modified input group, the students listened to a script read by a native speaker. The script had been simplified in a number of ways to facilitate comprehension. For example, there were repetition and paraphrasing, simple grammatical constructions and vocabulary, and so on. In the modified interaction group, the learners listened to a script which contained the same information, but which had *not* been simplified in any way. Instead, as learners listened to the script being read, they were encouraged to ask questions and seek verbal assistance when they had any difficulty following the directions.

Learners who had the opportunity to engage in interaction—ask clarification questions, and check their comprehension as they were listening to the instructions—comprehended much more than the students who received a simplified set of instructions to do the task but had no opportunity to interact while completing it.

Study 8: Interaction and second language development

Alison Mackey (1999) carried out one of the few studies which has directly examined the effects of different types of interaction behaviours on second language learning. In this study, adult learners of ESL were involved in different communicative tasks with native speakers of the target language. The tasks were designed to provide contexts for learners to produce question forms.

Group 1 included learners who interacted with native speakers. In these interactions, input was modified as the participants sought to clarify their meaning. Learners in group 2 did not engage in conversational interactions with native speakers. Instead they observed the interactions between the learners and native speakers in group 1. Group 3 included learners and native speakers who participated in the same communicative tasks as group 1, but the input the learners received was premodified. That is, the native speakers used language which had been simplified and scripted to match a level of language which was comprehensible to the learners. There was no negotiation of meaning between speakers in this group. The results indicated that learners who engaged in conversational interactions produced more advanced question forms than learners in the two other experimental groups.

Study 9: Interaction with recasts
In another study, Alison Mackey and Jenefer Philp (1998) looked again at the development of question forms in relation to negotiated interaction. In this research, the focus was on a particular feature of interaction, recasts. As described in Chapter 5, recasts are paraphrases of a learner's incorrect utterance which involve changing one or more components of the utterance while maintaining the meaning. In their study, Mackey and Philp were interested in discovering whether adult learners who received interactionally modified input *with* recasts were able to advance in their immediate production of question forms more than learners who received interactionally modified input *without* recasts. The results showed that learners who were at more advanced stages of question development benefited more from interaction with recasts than they did from interaction without recasts. Learners who were at less advanced stages of question development did not differ according to the type of interaction they were exposed to.

Interpreting the research

The research described above (and other related research) investigating the factors which contribute to the quality and quantity of interactions between second language learners has provided some very useful information for teaching. Certainly, the early work of Long and his colleagues (1976) and the findings of Porter (1986), and of Yule and Macdonald (1990) have contributed to a better understanding of how to organize group and pair work more effectively in the classroom.

The Mackey and Mackey and Philp studies are among the few which have been designed to measure second language development in relation to different aspects of conversational interaction. However, the measure of second language learning in both studies was the learners' immediate production following these interactions. It is therefore difficult to draw any conclusions as to the long-term benefits of conversational interaction. Furthermore, because these studies were designed as one-on-one pair-work activities between trained native speakers and non-native speakers focusing on a single grammatical feature, it is also difficult to relate the findings to the kind of interactions which take place in classrooms.

Some have argued that while recasts may contribute positively to learners' immediate production in pair-work situations, they are less likely to be effective in regular second language classrooms. Recasts may be more salient in pair work, particularly if only one form is recast consistently. In the second language classroom, however, teachers' recasts are not usually focused on only one form. Furthermore, when the instructional focus is on expressing meaning through subject-matter instruction, the teachers' recasts may not be perceived by the learners as an attempt to correct their language form but rather as just another way of saying the same thing (see Chapter 5, pages 103–6, and Lyster 1998 for further discussion).

3 Just listen . . . and read

This proposal is based on the assumption that it is not necessary to drill and memorize language forms in order to learn them. However, unlike the inter-actionists' emphasis on providing opportunities for interaction of the kind we saw in some of the excerpts in the 'Say what you mean and mean what you say' proposal, the emphasis here is on providing comprehensible input through listening and/or reading activities.

Read example 8 to get a feel for how this theory of classroom second language learning can be implemented.

Example 8

It is the English period at a primary school in a French-speaking area of New Brunswick, Canada. Students (aged 9–10) enter the classroom, which looks very much like a miniature language lab, with individual work spaces arranged around the perimeter of the room. They go to the shelves containing books and audio-cassettes and select the material which they wish to read and listen to during the next 30 minutes. For some of the time the teacher is walking around the classroom, checking that the machines are running smoothly. She does not interact with the students concerning what they are doing. Some of the students are listening with closed eyes; others read actively, pronouncing the words silently. The classroom is almost silent except for the sound of tapes being inserted or removed or chairs scraping as students go to the shelves to select new tapes and books.

'Just listen . . . and read' is one of the most influential and most controversial approaches to second language teaching because it not only says that second language learners need not drill and practise language in order to learn it, but also that they do not need to speak at all, except to get other people to speak to them. According to this view, it is enough to hear and understand the target language. And, as you saw in the classroom description above, one way to do this is to provide learners with a steady diet of listening and reading comprehension activities with no (or very few) opportunities to speak or interact with the teacher or other learners in the classroom.

The material which the students read and listen to is not graded in any rigid way according to a sequence of linguistic simplicity. Rather, the program planners grade materials on the basis of what they consider intuitively to be at an appropriate level for the different groups of learners, because a given text has shorter sentences, clearer illustrations, or is based on a theme or topic that is familiar to the learners.

As noted in Chapter 2, the individual whose name is most closely associated with this proposal is Stephen Krashen, particularly with his hypothesis that the one essential requirement for second language acquisition is the availability of comprehensible input (Krashen 1985).

Research findings

Several studies which are relevant to this proposal include: (1) research in experimental *comprehension-based* ESL programs in Canada; (2) research investigating the effects of the 'Total physical response' method of second language teaching; (3) research in Canadian French immersion programs; and (4) research which manipulates the input to learners in different ways.

Study 10: Comprehension-based instruction for children

Example 8 was a description of a real program which was developed in experimental classes in a French-speaking region in Canada. From the beginning of their ESL instruction in grade 3 (aged 8), these francophone students only listen and read during their daily 30-minute ESL period. There is no oral practice or interaction in English at all. Teachers do not 'teach' but provide organizational and technical support. Thus, learners receive native-speaker input from tapes and books but virtually no interaction with the teacher or other learners.

Patsy Lightbown and Randall Halter investigated the second language development of hundreds of children in this program and compared these findings with the second language development of those in the regular, aural-oral ESL program. All the students (experimental and comparison) began learning ESL at grade 3 and the study reported on their performance at grade 5. Their results revealed that learners in the comprehension-based program learned English as well as (and in some cases better than) learners in the regular program through grade 5 (Lightbown 1992). This was true not only for their comprehension skills but also for their speaking skills. This comes as something of a surprise since the learners in the innovative programs *never* practised spoken English in their classes. However, a follow-up study in grade 8 revealed that students who continued in the comprehension-only program were not doing as well as students in a program that included speaking and writing components, teacher feedback, and classroom interaction.

Study 11: Total physical response

One of the best-known variations on the 'Just listen . . . and read' proposal is the second language teaching approach called 'Total physical response' (TPR). In TPR classes, students—children or adults—participate in activities in which they hear a series of commands in the target language, for example: 'stand up', 'sit down', 'pick up the book', 'put the book on the table', 'walk to the door'. For a substantial number of hours of instruction, students are not required to say anything. They simply listen and show their comprehension by their actions. This instruction differs from the comprehension-based instruction described in study 8 and from Krashen's theoretical version of 'Just listen . . . and read' in an important way: the vocabulary and structures which learners are exposed to are carefully graded and organized so that learners deal with material which gradually increases in complexity and each new lesson builds on the ones before. Krashen, of course, would not recommend structural grading but only that teachers modify their speech to ensure students' comprehension.

TPR was developed by James Asher, whose research has shown that students can develop quite advanced levels of comprehension in the language without engaging in oral practice (Asher 1972). When students begin to speak, they take over the role of the teacher and give commands as well as following them. It is clear that there are limitations on the kind of language students can learn in such an environment. Nevertheless, Asher's research shows that, for beginners, this kind of active listening gives learners a good start. It allows them to build up a considerable knowledge of the language without feeling the nervousness that often accompanies the first attempts to speak the new language.

Study 12: French immersion programs in Canada

Other research which is often cited as relevant to the 'Just listen . . . and read' proposal comes from Canadian French immersion programs, which have been described by Krashen as communicative language teaching *par excellence*. The reason for this is that the focus in French immersion is on meaning through subject-matter instruction and the provision of rich, comprehensible input. In many ways, Krashen could not have asked for a better laboratory to test his theory. What have the studies shown?

First, there is little doubt that the overall findings provide convincing evidence that these programs are among the most successful large-scale second language programs in existence. Learners develop fluency, functional abilities, and confidence in using their second language. There is, however, a growing awareness that French immersion learners fail to achieve high levels of performance in some aspects of French grammar even after several years of full-day exposure to the second language in these programs (Harley and Swain 1984). There are several possible explanations for this.

Some researchers argue very explicitly that French immersion shows that comprehensible input is not enough. They believe that the learners engage in too little language production because the classes are largely teacher-centred. Students speak relatively little and are rarely required to give extended answers (Swain 1985). This permits students to operate successfully with their incomplete knowledge of the language because they are rarely pushed to be more precise or more accurate. When students do speak, communication is quite satisfactory in spite of numerous errors in their speech. Because students share the same interlanguage, they have no difficulty understanding each other. Teachers are also very capable of understanding the students. Therefore, there is little need for negotiation of meaning.

Other observers have suggested that the students need more *form-focused* instruction. This is based partly on experimental studies in which the addition of form-focused instruction in French immersion classes has been shown to benefit learners (see studies 22, 23 and 24 under the 'Get it right in the end' proposal, pages 146–8). It has also been observed that certain linguistic features rarely or never appear in the language of the teacher or the students in these content-based instructional environments (Swain, 1988). Furthermore, the presence in the classroom of other learners whose interlanguages are influenced by the same first language, the same learning environment, and the same limited contact with the target language outside the classroom, makes it difficult for an individual learner to work out how his or her own use of the language differs from the target language.

Other more recent studies which explore the 'Just listen . . . and read' position include 'input flood', 'enhanced input', and 'input processing' studies. In this research, efforts have been made to draw the second language learners' attention to language forms in different ways, for example, providing learners with high-frequency exposure to specific language features, enhancing the features in some way, and/or providing explicit instruction. The emphasis in all cases, however, is on getting the learners to notice language forms in the input, not on getting them to practise producing the forms.

Study 13: Input flood
Martha Trahey and Lydia White (1993) carried out a study with young francophone learners (aged 10–12) in intensive ESL classes in Quebec. The goal of this research was to determine whether high-frequency exposure to a particular form in the instructional input would lead to better knowledge and use of that form by the students. The linguistic form investigated was adverb placement in English (see Chapter 4, Table 4.3 (page 87) to see how English and French rules differ). For approximately 10 hours over a two-week period, learners read a series of short texts in which they were exposed to literally hundreds of instances of adverbs in English sentences—so many that the investigators referred to this study as an 'input flood'. There was no teaching of

adverb placement nor was any error correction given. Instead, students simply read the passages and completed a variety of comprehension activities based on them.

The results showed that although learners benefited from this exposure to sentences with adverbs in all the correct positions, their knowledge was incomplete. Learners developed a better understanding of what was grammatical in English adverb placement (for example, they could correctly place adverbs at the beginning and end of sentences like 'Quickly the children leave school' or 'The children leave school quickly') and they learned that English, unlike French, allows the adverb between the subject and the verb ('The children quickly leave school'). However, they continued to view sentences such as 'The children leave quickly school' as correct. This assumption is based on the fact that in French, it is grammatically acceptable to place an adverb between the verb and the direct object. The students' inability to recognize that adverbs in this position are ungrammatical in English suggests that exposure to many instances of correct models in the instructional input could help them add something new to their interlanguage, but not to get rid of an error based on their first language. Lydia White (1987) has argued that although exposure to language input may provide learners with information about what *is* possible in the second language, it fails to provide them with information about what is *not possible*. Thus, more explicit information about what is not grammatical in the second language may be necessary for particular features in the learners' continued development. This is discussed in more detail in the section 'Get it right in the end'.

Study 14: Enhanced input

A related study with learners in intensive ESL classes was carried out by Joanna White (1998). She examined the acquisition of possessive determiners (for example, his/her), also through an input flood. Learners in grade 6 (aged 11–12 years) received approximately ten hours of exposure to hundreds of possessive determiners through a package of reading materials and comprehension activities provided over a two-week period. The major difference between this study and that of Trahey and White described above is that the reading passages were designed to draw the learners' attention to the possessive determiners which were embedded in the texts. This was done through typographical enhancement. That is, every time a possessive determiner appeared in the texts, it was either in **bold type**, underlined, *italicized*, or written in CAPITAL LETTERS. The assumption was that this would lead the learners to notice the possessive determiners in the midst of all the other language input.

Comparison of the performance of learners who had read the typographically enhanced passages with that of learners who read the texts without enhancement, showed little difference in their knowledge and use of these forms. In interpreting her results, White questions whether the enhancement was sufficiently explicit to draw the learners' attention to possessive determiners.

Enhancing the input

Study 15: Input processing

In a series of studies, Bill VanPatten and his colleagues (VanPatten and Cadierno 1993, VanPatten and Sanz 1995) have investigated whether guided and more directed exposure to language forms in the input can lead learners to higher levels of knowledge and performance. In this research, adult learners of Spanish as a second language received instruction on different linguistic forms, for example, object pronouns. VanPatten had found that English-speaking learners of Spanish tended to treat the object pronouns which precede the verb in Spanish as if they were subject pronouns. Thus, a sentence such as 'La sigue el señor' [literally 'her (object) follows the man (subject)'] was interpreted as 'She follows the man.'

One group of learners received explicit explanations about object pronouns, as well as strictly comprehension-based practice. That is, through a variety of focused listening and reading activities, learners were required to pay attention to how the target forms were used in order to convey meaning. For example, they heard or read a sentence such as 'La sigue el señor' and had to choose which picture—a man following a woman or a woman following a man—corresponded to the sentence. VanPatten calls this 'processing instruction'. A second group of learners also received explicit information about the target forms but instead of processing instruction, they engaged in production practice, doing exercises to practise the forms being taught.

After the instruction, learners who had received the comprehension-based processing instruction not only achieved higher levels of performance on the comprehension tasks than learners in the production group, they also performed as well on production tasks.

Interpreting the research

The results of the French immersion research confirm the effectiveness of comprehensible input. Students develop not only good comprehension (in reading and listening), but also confidence and fluency in French. However, research does not support the argument that an exclusive focus on meaning in comprehensible input is enough to bring learners to high levels of accuracy in their second language. Indeed, the fact that French immersion learners continue to make the same linguistic errors after years of exposure to the second language in classrooms which provide a great deal of comprehensible input is a challenge to the claim that language will take care of itself as long as meaningful comprehensible input is provided.

The results of the research on comprehension-based ESL in Canada also provide some support for Krashen's comprehensible input hypothesis. It is important to keep in mind that the learners in the comprehension-based studies were beginner-level learners and the follow-up study suggested that more guidance from a teacher was needed to ensure that their second language skills continued to develop. Learners in these comprehension-based programs, like the French immersion learners, had considerable gaps in their linguistic knowledge and performance. And their performance was eventually surpassed by that of students who had opportunities to use the language interactively and to receive some careful form-focused intervention later in their development.

The TPR results also show great benefits for learners in the early stages of development. Krashen says of TPR that it prepares learners to go out into the target-language community to get *more* comprehensible input which, he says, will carry their language acquisition further.

The input flood and enhancement studies provide further evidence that second language learners may not be able to discover what is ungrammatical in their own interlanguage if the focus is always on meaning, even if the frequency and salience of correct models is increased.

The results of the 'processing instruction' studies show greater benefits for comprehension practice over production practice. However, this research points to the benefits of a focus on language form *within* input-based instruction. In this approach, learners' attention was drawn explicitly to form–meaning relationships.

In summary, comprehension-based programs appear to be beneficial in the development of basic comprehension and communicative performance in the early stages of learning (particularly in situations where learners have no other contact with the target language apart from in classroom situations). But they may not be sufficient to get learners to continue developing their second language abilities to advanced levels. In particular, comprehension-based instruction may make it difficult for learners to discover and eliminate patterns already present in their interlanguage that are not grammatical in the target language.

4 *Teach what is teachable*

The researcher most closely associated with this view is Manfred Pienemann. He and his associates tried to explain why it often seems that some things can be taught successfully whereas other things, even after extensive or intensive teaching, seem to remain unacquired. Their research provides evidence that some linguistic structures, for example, basic sentence word order (both simple and complex) develops along a particular developmental path. These structures are called *developmental features*. The developmental stages of question formation which we saw in Chapter 4 are based on this research. Pienemann claims that any attempt to teach a 'stage 4' word-order pattern to learners at 'stage 1' will not work because learners have to pass through 'stage 2' and get to 'stage 3' before they are ready to acquire what is at 'stage 4'. (See Pienemann 1985, Pienemann, Johnston, and Brindley 1988.)

The underlying cause of the stages has not been fully explained, but there has been considerable research showing that they may be based at least in part on learners' developing ability to process (unconsciously analyse and organize) certain elements in the stream of speech they hear.

Researchers supporting this view also claim that certain other aspects of language—for example, vocabulary—can be taught at any time. A learner's success in learning these *variational features* will depend on factors such as motivation, intelligence, and the quality of instruction.

While this line of research has the potential to inform classroom teachers about which language features are 'developmental' (and thus teachable only in a given sequence) and which are 'variational' (and thus teachable at various points in learner language development), there is much work to be done before the findings of this research can lead to recommendations about whether particular forms can be taught and when.

In example 9 below, we see a teacher trying to help students with question formation. The students seem to know what the teacher means, but the level of language the teacher is offering them is beyond their current stage of development. A look back at Chapter 4 will show you how far the students are from where the teacher would like them to be. The students react by simply answering the question or accepting the teacher's formulation.

Example 9

Students in intensive ESL (11–12-year-old French speakers) interviewing a student who had been in the same class in a previous year—see Transcript 1 in Chapter 5, pp. 107–8.

> S1 Mylène, where you put your 'Kid of the Week' poster?
> T   Where *did* you put your poster when you got it?
> S2 In my room.
> (two minutes later)
> S3 Beatrice, where you put your 'Kid of the Week' poster?
> T   Where *did* you put your poster?
> S4 My poster was on my wall and it fell down.

In example 10 below, the student is using a 'fronting' strategy which is typical of stage 3 learners. That is, the student simply places something (in this case 'is') at the beginning of the sentence but does not change the rest of the sentence. The teacher's correction leads the student to imitate a stage 4 question. In example 11, the same situation appears. This time, however, the correction leads not to an imitation or a reformulation of the question, but simply to an answer.

Example 10

(The same group of students engaged in 'Famous person' interviews.)

> S1 Is your mother play piano?
> T   'Is your mother play piano?'? OK. Well, can you say 'Is your mother play piano?' or 'Is your mother a piano player?'?
> S1 'Is your mother a piano player?'
> S2 No.

Example 11

(Interviewing each other about house preferences.)

> S1 Is your favourite house is a split-level?
> S2 Yes.
> T   You're saying 'is' two times dear. 'Is your favourite house a split-level?'
> S1 A split-level.
> T   OK.

Example 12

('Hide and seek' game.)

> S   Where the teacher books are?
> T   Where are the teacher's books?
> S   Where are the tea—the teacher books?

In example 12 the student asks a stage 3 question, the teacher provides a stage 4 correction, and the student is able to imitate the stage 4 question. Note, however, that the student still does not pronounce the possessive *'s*, something which French speakers find very difficult.

Research findings

The 'Teach what is teachable' view is one which claims that while some features of the language can be taught successfully at various points in the learners' development, other features develop according to the learners' internal schedule. It also claims that although learners may be able to produce more advanced forms on tests or in very restricted pedagogical exercises, instruction cannot change the 'natural' developmental course. The recommendation is to assess the learners' developmental level and teach what would naturally come next. Let us examine some studies which have tested this hypothesis.

Study 16: Ready to learn

In a study of the acquisition of German as a second language, Manfred Pienemann (1988) investigated whether instruction permitted learners to 'skip' a stage in the natural sequence of development. Two groups of Australian university students who were at stage 2 in their acquisition of German word order were taught the rules associated with stage 3 and stage 4 respectively. The instruction took place over two weeks and during this time learners were provided with explicit grammatical rules and exercises for stage 4 constructions. The results showed that the learners who received instruction on stage 3 rules moved easily into this stage from stage 2. However, those learners who received instruction on stage 4 rules did not move into this stage. They either continued to use stage 2 behaviours or they moved into stage 3. That is, they were not able to 'skip' a stage in the developmental sequence. Pienemann interprets his results as support for the hypothesis that for some linguistic structures, learners cannot be taught what they are not 'developmentally ready' to learn.

Study 17: Teaching when the time is right

Catherine Doughty (1991) examined whether particular aspects of relative clause formation would benefit from instruction at a time when learners were developmentally 'ready' to learn them. Twenty adult university students of English as a second language were divided into three groups: two experimental and one control. On the basis of a placement test, Doughty concluded that all learners were developmentally ready to acquire relative clauses. All groups received exposure to relative clauses over a period of ten days through a series of computer-delivered reading lessons. During these lessons all learners were asked to read the passages and answer a variety of comprehension questions which focused on reading skills such as skimming and scanning.

For the experimental groups, two instructional techniques were added to the reading comprehension exercises. These were presented to the learners by means of an additional 'window' on the learners' computer screens. One experimental group received instruction which clarified the meaning of the relative clauses. This included both vocabulary assistance and paraphrases of sentences in the reading comprehension texts. The other experimental group received instruction which focused on rules for forming relative clauses. This included a combination of explicit grammatical rules and on-screen sentence manipulation. The control group simply read the sentences containing relative clauses and answered the comprehension questions.

All learners were pre-tested immediately before the instructional treatment and post-tested after ten days of the exposure/instruction with regard to relative clauses.

The results revealed a clear advantage for both experimental groups compared to the control group. That is, learners who had received the additional instruction in relative clause formation—regardless of whether it was meaning-focused or rule-focused—outperformed the control group. Doughty concludes that instruction on relative clauses made a difference when it was provided at the time when learners were 'developmentally ready' to learn them.

Study 18: Can question forms be taught?

Rod Ellis (1984) studied the effects of instruction on the acquisition of question forms by 13 ESL learners (aged 11–15). In this study, learners were given instruction at a time when they were considered to be 'developmentally ready' to acquire *wh-* question inversion rules. Their 'readiness' was assessed on the basis of classroom observations which revealed that they had begun to ask questions, including *wh-* questions, but that they had not mastered rules for inversion. The learners received three hours of instruction. In the first hour the teacher asked a series of *wh-* questions while referring to a wall poster, and students were asked to respond. In the second hour, the students asked questions (again referring to the wall poster), and the teacher corrected them when they made errors. In the third hour, the teacher 'fired questions at the pupils' about the wall poster.

After the instruction, students participated in a oral activity in which they asked questions prompted by a picture of a classroom scene and cue cards with *wh-* words on them. The group results showed little effect for instruction on the learners' development of question forms, although some individual learners did improve substantially.

Study 19: Developmental stage and the influence of the first language

In our own work, we have also investigated the acquisition of questions in relation to learners' developmental 'readiness' (Spada and Lightbown 1999). In this study, students (aged 11–12) in intensive ESL classes received high-frequency exposure to question forms which were one or two stages beyond their developmental stage. Learners who were judged on oral pre-tests to be at stage 2 or 3 in their question formation were given high frequency exposure to stage 4 and 5 questions in the instructional input.

The materials which contained the more advanced question forms were designed to engage the learners in primarily receptive practice. There was no student production and thus no corrective feedback, nor was there any explicit instruction on question formation. We were interested in discovering whether stage 3 learners (i.e. those considered to be developmentally 'ready') would benefit more from the high frequency exposure to stage 4 and 5 questions than the stage 2 learners (i.e. those who were *not* yet developmentally 'ready').

Learners' performance on the oral post-test measure indicated no advantage for the stage 3 learners. In fact, there was little progress for either group. However, on one of the written measures (i.e. the preference task), there was evidence that all students had some knowledge of stage 4 and 5 questions. A more detailed examination of the learners' performance on this task showed that students tended to accept stage 4 and 5 questions when the subject of the sentence was a pronoun (for example, 'Are you a good student?' 'When are you going to eat breakfast?'). When the subject of the sentence was a noun, however, there was a tendency for students to reject higher stage questions (for example, 'Are the students watching TV?' 'What is your brother doing?'). As we saw in Chapter 4, this pattern in the students' performance appears to be directly tied to a question formation rule in their first language. That is, in French, questions with nouns in subject position are *not* inverted (for example, *'Peut-Jean venir chez moi?' = 'Can John come to my house?') In French questions with pronoun subjects, however, inversion is permitted (for example, 'Peut-il venir chez moi?' = 'Can he come to my house?').

These results indicate that instruction which is timed to match learners' developmental 'readiness' may move them into more advanced stages but their performance may still be affected by other factors. In this study first language influence seems to be responsible for the learners' inability to generalize their knowledge of inversion to all questions.

Interpreting the research

The results of these studies present several problems for assessing the 'Teach what is teachable' proposal. A closer look at some of the procedural problems in the research should shed some light on the seemingly contradictory findings. It seems possible, for example, that the three hours provided in the Ellis study were not enough to cause changes in learners' interlanguage systems. Further, there is the possibility that the type of instruction was not sufficiently form-focused. There was no explicit instruction. In addition, in the limited description of the type of instruction provided in Ellis's study, it seems that the learners had exposure to *wh*-questions in the teacher's modelling but few opportunities to produce questions themselves and to receive feedback on their errors. Furthermore, in contrast to the type of attentive listening required for input processing or TPR instruction, students in these studies could perform classroom tasks successfully without having to notice exactly how the teacher's sentences (questions, in this case) were formed.

The Spada and Lightbown study also did not include any explicit instruction in the formation of questions. Learners were simply exposed to a high frequency of correctly formed higher stage questions in the input. In this way, the learners may have been more similar to those involved in the input flood experiments or the control group in Doughty's study: they received increased 'exposure' but not much 'instruction' and in the end did not perform as well as those learners who received more focused instruction. Explicit instruction might have led to more positive results, particularly if the instruction had consisted of contrastive information about inversion in English versus French questions with regard to nouns and pronouns.

It seems reasonable to conclude that, because the instruction provided to the experimental groups in the Doughty and Pienemann studies was more explicit, their studies provide a more reliable test of the 'Teach what is teachable' proposal. Nonetheless, it is important to note some of the weaknesses in these studies as a test of this position. For example, in Doughty's, no direct comparison was made between learners who were *not* 'developmentally ready' to learn relative clauses and those who *were*. Further, in both studies, only the short-term effects of instruction were measured. Because of this, there is no way of knowing whether instruction had any permanent or long-term effects on the learners' developing interlanguage systems. In Pienemann's study, results were reported for only a small group of learners. In later studies, however, similar results were reported with other learners.

In concluding this section, it is important to note that there is other research which is sometimes said to offer counter-evidence to the claim that it is beneficial to teach what is developmentally next. For example, a series of studies have used the Accessibility Hierarchy for relative clauses in English (see Chapter 4, Table 4.2, page 83) to determine second language learners' progress in their acquisition of relative clauses. Several researchers have reported that when low-level learners (for example, learners using relative clauses only in subject position) are taught relative clauses which are several stages beyond their current level, they not only learn what is taught, they also acquire the relative clause position between the one taught and the one(s) they already knew. In some instances they even learn how to use relative clauses *beyond* the level they were taught (see Eckman, Bell, and Nelson 1988; Hamilton 1994).

On the surface, these findings appear to contradict Pienemann's claim that learners should be taught what is 'next'. However, it is also possible that the basis for the developmental paths of different linguistic features varies. Doughty suggests, for example, that once learners have learned to use relative clauses in one position (usually the subject position), there is no constraint on their ability to learn the others. What all the studies of relative clause teaching and learning have in common is that learners acquire the relative clauses in an order very similar to the accessibility hierarchy. That is, whether or not they learn what is taught, they make progress by learning subject, then direct object, then indirect object, and so on.

Clearly, the 'Teach what is teachable' position is of great potential interest to syllabus planners as well as teachers. Future research will help to determine the extent to which developmental sequences need to be taken into account in planning lessons and materials for second language learning.

5 Get it right in the end

Proponents of the 'Get it right in the end' position recognize an important role for form-focused instruction, but they do not assume that everything has to be taught. Like advocates of the 'Say what you mean and mean what you say' and the 'Just listen . . . and read' positions, they have concluded that many language features—from pronunciation to vocabulary and grammar— will be acquired naturally if learners have adequate exposure to the language and a motivation to learn. Thus, while they view comprehension-based, content-based, task-based, or other types of essentially meaning-focused instruction as crucial for language learning, they hypothesize that learners will do better if they also have access to some form-focused instruction. They argue that learners will benefit in terms of both speed and efficiency of their learning and also in terms of the level of proficiency which they will eventually reach.

Proponents of this position also agree with advocates of the 'Teach what is teachable' position that some things cannot be taught if the teaching fails to take the student's readiness (stage of development) into account. This proposal differs from the 'Teach what is teachable' proposal, however, in that it emphasizes the idea that some aspects of language *must* be taught and may need to be taught quite explicitly. There are a number of situations in which guidance— form-focused instruction or corrective feedback—are expected to be especially desirable. For example, when learners in a class share the same first language and make an error that is the result of transfer from that shared language then all the learners in a group will tend to make the same error, and since the error is not likely to lead to any kind of communication breakdown, it will be virtually impossible for learners to discover the error on their own. We can see this in example 13, where francophone learners of English are having difficulties with adverb placement.

Example 13

Examples 13, 14, and 15 are taken from a classroom where a group of 12-year-olds are learning English. In example 13, they are engaged in an activity where scrambled sentences are reordered to form sensible ones. The following sentence has been placed on the board: 'Sometimes my mother makes good cakes.'

> T   Another place to put our adverb?
> S1 After *makes*?
> T   After *makes*.
> S2 Before *good*?
> T   *My mother makes sometimes good cakes.*
> S3 No.
> T   No, we can't do that. It sounds yucky.
> S3 Yucky!
> T   Disgusting. Horrible. Right?
> S4 Horrible!

This hardly a typical grammar lesson! And yet the students' attention is being drawn to an error virtually all of them (native speakers of French) make in English.

'Get it right in the end' also differs from 'Just listen . . . and read' in that it is assumed that learners will need some guidance in learning some specific features of the target language. Furthermore, it is assumed that what learners learn when they are focusing on language itself *can* eventually lead to changes in their interlanguage systems, not just to an appearance of change brought about by conscious attention to a few details of form. On the other hand, the supporters of this proposal do not claim that teaching particular language points will prevent learners from making errors. Nor do they assume that learners will be able to begin using a form or structure with complete accuracy as soon as it is taught. Furthermore, they do not argue that the focused teaching must always be done in a way which involves explicit *explanations* of the point or that learners need to be able to *explain* why something is right or wrong. Rather, they claim that the learners' attention must be *focused on* how their language use differs from that of a more proficient speaker. As we will see in the examples below, teachers must look for the right moment to create increased awareness on the part of the learner—ideally, at a time when the learner is motivated to say something and wants to say it as clearly and correctly as possible.

Example 14

(The students are practising following instructions; one student instructs, others colour.)

> S1 Make her shoes brown.
> T   Now, *her* shoes. Are those Mom's shoes or Dad's shoes?

S2 Mom's.
T Mom's. How do you know it's Mom's?
S1 Because it's *her* shoes.

French-speaking learners of English have difficulty with *his* and *her* because French possessives use the grammatical gender of the object possessed rather than the natural gender of the possessor in selecting the appropriate possessive form. The teacher is aware of this and—briefly, without interrupting the activity—helps the learners 'notice' the correct form.

Example 15
(The students are playing 'hide and seek' with a doll in a doll's house, asking questions until they find out where 'George' is hiding.)

S1 Is George is in the living room?
T You said 'is' two times dear. Listen to you—you said 'Is George is in?' Look on the board. 'Is George in the' and then you say the name of the room.
S1 Is George in the living room?
T Yeah.
S1 I win!

Note that the teacher's brief correction does not distract the student from his pleasure in the game, demonstrating that focus on form does not have to interfere with genuine interaction.

Proponents of 'Get it right in the end' argue that it is sometimes necessary to draw learners' attention to their errors and to focus on certain linguistic (vocabulary or grammar) points. However, it is different from the 'Get it right from the beginning' proposal in acknowledging that it is appropriate for learners to engage in meaningful language use from the very beginning of their exposure to the second language. They assume that much of language acquisition will develop naturally out of such language use, without formal instruction which focuses on the language itself.

This proposal differs from the 'Just listen . . . and read' and 'Say what you mean and mean what you say' proposals because it is not assumed that comprehensible input and meaningful interaction will be enough to bring learners to high levels of accuracy as well as fluency. Researchers who support this proposal argue that learners can benefit from, and sometimes require, explicit focus on the language.

Research findings

In recent years, there has been an increasing interest in examining issues related to this proposal, leading to both *descriptive* and *experimental studies*.

Study 20: Attention to form in communicative ESL

Nina Spada (1987) examined the effects of differences in instruction on the English language proficiency of 48 adult learners enrolled in a six-week intensive course. All learners received communicative instruction, that is, instruction which focused primarily on meaning-based practice and opportunities to use the second language in creative and spontaneous ways. However, some teachers focused more on grammar than others. For example, the teacher in class A spent considerably more time teaching grammar than did the teachers in classes B and C. In class B, the students' attention was frequently drawn to specific linguistic features, but this was done while students were engaged in communicative activities, not as a separate lesson. In class C, attention was rarely, if ever, drawn to specific linguistic features.

The learners were given a number of proficiency tests before and after instruction. This included: (1) a listening comprehension test; (2) a reading comprehension test; (3) an oral interview/interaction task; (4) a multiple-choice grammar test; (5) a multiple-choice discourse test; and (6) a sociolinguistic test.

The results showed that learners in class A (the ones who received more grammatical instruction) performed slightly better on the grammar test than learners in classes B and C. Furthermore, the results indicated that learners in class A improved more than the other classes on some of the other measures as well (listening, speaking, and discourse tests). It was particularly interesting to note that learners in class B performed best in terms of both accuracy and fluency on the oral interview/interaction task. In this class, students were often encouraged to pay attention to the formal aspects of their speech while they were engaged in communicative practice. Spada concluded that instruction which focuses primarily on meaning (i.e. is communication-based), but allows for a focus on form within meaningful contexts, works best.

Study 21: Form-focus experiments in ESL

In Quebec, we have investigated the effects of form-focused instruction and corrective feedback on the development of specific linguistic structures in the English of francophone students participating in intensive ESL programs for five months in grade 5 or 6 (aged 10–12).

According to the findings of a descriptive study involving almost 1,000 students in 33 classes, these programs can be considered to be essentially communicative. There is no structural syllabus for these classes, and language features tend to be learned as they come up in communicative interaction. The emphasis of the teaching is on activities which focus on meaning rather than form, opportunities for spontaneous interaction, and the provision of rich and varied comprehensible input. Learners develop listening comprehension, fluency, and communicative ability in English, but they still have problems with linguistic accuracy and complexity (Lightbown and Spada 1994).

The experimental studies involved a smaller number of classes. In these studies, the effects of form-focused instruction and corrective feedback on two particular linguistic features were examined: adverb placement and question formation. In the first study, Lydia White selected adverb placement for investigation because of the differences between English and French which have been discussed (see study 13 in 'Just listen . . . and read', pages 131–2). The hypothesis was that learners would persist in using adverb placement rules consistent with French (their first language) if they were not explicitly told how rules for adverb placement differ in English and French. Questions were selected for the second study because they have been extensively investigated in the literature and considerable comparison data are available, particularly with regard to acquisition sequences.

Both the experimental and the comparison groups were tested before the experiment began (pre-test), and both groups were tested again when the period of special instruction had ended (post-test). The experimental groups received approximately eight hours of instruction over a two-week period. This included some explicit teaching of the grammatical rules associated with each structure as well as corrective feedback. The teachers of the experimental groups were provided with a package of teaching materials and a clear set of procedures to follow. The comparison group teachers were asked to teach a different structure, one which was not the focus of the experiment, so that the comparison group learners would be familiar with the tasks and activities that were used in the testing procedures. The studies included immediate, delayed, and long-term/follow-up post-tests. For the adverb study the test tasks were written, and in the question formation study the tests included both written and oral tasks.

The results of the adverb study revealed that learners who received instruction on adverb placement dramatically outperformed the learners who did not receive instruction on adverbs. This was found on all tests in both the immediate and delayed post-tests (immediately following instruction and six weeks later). In the follow-up tests a year later, however, the gains made by the learners who had received the adverb instruction had disappeared and their performance on this structure was like that of uninstructed learners (White 1991).

In the question formation study the instructed group also made significantly greater gains than the uninstructed group on the written tasks immediately following instruction. Furthermore, the instructed learners maintained their level of knowledge on later testing (six weeks and six months after instruction). Focus on form also contributed to improvements in oral performance on questions.

The difference in long-term effects of the two studies may be due to a difference in the availability of the target forms in the classroom input learners were exposed to. Analysis of classroom language showed that adverbs were extremely rare in classroom speech, giving learners little opportunity to maintain their newly acquired knowledge through continued exposure and use. In contrast, there were hundreds of opportunities to hear and use questions every day in the classroom. Once learners had been given some focused instruction, it seems they were able to continue to advance in their knowledge and use of questions (White, Spada, Lightbown and Ranta 1991; Spada and Lightbown 1993).

Study 22: Focusing on past tense forms in French immersion

As mentioned earlier in this chapter, there is a growing belief that learners in content-based programs such as French immersion programs need more opportunities to focus on form and receive corrective feedback. There has been a call for more classroom research of the type exemplified by studies 22, 23, and 24 to determine how this can best be accomplished.

Birgit Harley (1989) examined the effects of a functional approach to grammar teaching on a particularly problematic area of grammar for English-speaking learners of French—the contrastive use of two past tense forms: *imparfait* (roughly, the habitual or descriptive past, for example 'Ma mère *parlait* souvent de son enfance' [My mother often spoke about her childhood]), and *passé composé* (roughly the simple or narrative past, for example 'Hier *j'ai parlé* avec les autres élèves' [Yesterday I spoke with the other students]).

Grade 6 immersion students (aged 11–12) were given instruction on the use of these past tense forms through teaching materials which encouraged their use in a variety of function-based practice activities. No explicit grammatical rules were provided, nor was there an emphasis on corrective feedback. The intention was to create opportunities, activities, and tasks which would expose students to more input containing both verb forms, and encourage more productive use of both forms. The experimental teaching materials were used over an eight-week period. Learners were tested on their spoken and written knowledge of the *imparfait* and *passé composé* before the instructional treatment began, eight weeks later, and again three months later.

Harley found that learners in the experimental classes outperformed learners in the comparison classes on the immediate post-tests on some of the written and oral measures. Three months later there were no significant differences between the two groups. However, both had continued to improve, and Harley found that teachers in the comparison classes had spent a considerable amount of time focused on *passé composé*. Thus, this study seems to confirm the value of some guided practice with particular language forms within content-based instructional programs.

Study 23 Focusing on the conditional in French immersion

Elaine Day and Stan Shapson (1991) examined the effects of form-focused instruction with grade 7 students (age about 12 or 13) in French immersion. The feature of French grammar which was taught was the conditional mood of the verb, for example in sentences such as 'Si je gagnais la loterie, je *partirais* en voyage' (If I won the lottery, I *would go* away on a trip).

Students in the experimental classes received several hours of focused instruction on the conditional over a period of 5–7 weeks. The students in the control group continued with their usual classroom routines, that is, they continued to encounter French mainly in the context of learning their general school subjects (science, mathematics, history, etc. through the medium of French).

Special teaching materials were prepared for the experimental classes by the team of researchers. They consisted of: (1) group work which created situations for the use of the conditional in natural communicative situations; (2) written and oral exercises to reinforce the use of the conditional in more formal, structured situations; and (3) self-evaluation activities to encourage students to develop conscious awareness of their language use. Oral and written tests were administered before the instructional treatment, immediately after the instruction (five to seven weeks later), and at the end of the school year.

Learners in the experimental classes outperformed those in the control classes on the immediate post-tests for the written, but not the oral, tasks. They were still doing better than the control group on the follow-up post-tests administered several months later.

Study 24: Focusing on sociolinguistic forms in French immersion

Roy Lyster (1994), also working in French immersion programs, carried out a study which examined the effects of form-focused instruction on the knowledge and use of sociolinguistic style variations in three classes of grade 8 French immersion students (about 13 years old). One of the main features examined in his study was the distinction between the use of second person singular forms *tu* and *vous* in French. The former is used to indicate informality and familiarity while the latter is used as a formal marker of politeness. Prior to instruction, immediately after, and again one month later, the learners were tested on their ability to produce and recognize these forms (in addition to others) in appropriate contexts.

The instruction took place for an average of 12 hours over a five-week period. During this time, students in the experimental classes were given explicit instruction in sociostylistic variation and engaged in guided practice activities that included role plays in a variety of formal and informal contexts and corrective feedback from teachers and peers. Students in the two comparison classes continued with their regular instruction without any focused instruction or guided practice in using sociolinguistically appropriate forms. On the immediate post-test, learners in the experimental classes significantly out-performed learners in the comparison classes on both written and oral production tasks and the multiple-choice test. Furthermore, these benefits were maintained when learners were tested a month later.

Study 25: Focusing on verb form in content-based science classrooms

Catherine Doughty and Elizabeth Varela (1998) carried out a study with a group of ESL learners who also received second language instruction via content-based teaching. One class of middle-school students (11–14 years old) from a variety of first language backgrounds received corrective feedback on past tense and conditional verb forms in English in their science class. That is, while they were engaged in oral and written work related to a series of science reports, the teacher corrected their errors in past tense and conditional forms—both explicitly and implicitly. Students were tested on their knowledge of these verb forms prior to the experiment and they were post-tested six weeks later and again two months later. Their performance was compared to that of a group of students who were in another science class doing the same science reports but who did not receive corrective feedback on past tense forms. The results showed that students who received the corrective feedback had made more progress in using past and conditional forms than the comparison group on both the immediate and delayed post-tests.

Study 26: Focusing on form in learner–learner interaction

Most of the research which has examined the potential benefits of drawing the learners' attention to language form has been done in teacher-centred classrooms. However, some work has investigated whether learners can provide each other with information about language (and corrective feedback) when interacting in group work. For example, recent work has been carried out to explore the Vygotskyan notion that learners can make progress in the second language through collaborative interaction. Maria Kowal and Merrill Swain (1994) asked students (about 13 years old) in a grade 8 French immersion class to participate in a paired task which led them to focus on form. In this type of task, referred to as dictogloss (Wajnryb 1990), students listen to a short but dense passage which is read twice at normal speed. While they listen, they take notes, and later they work in pairs or groups to reconstruct the passage. In this study, students completed four dictoglosses over a two-month period. In order to reconstruct the passages, they had to pay attention to how their meaning was expressed and to prepare their text so that it could be assessed by the whole class afterwards. The results of the study showed that students were successful in providing each other with information about language form and corrective feedback while engaged in a communicative task.

Interpreting the research

The overall results of the studies described above provide support for the hypothesis that form-focused instruction and corrective feedback within communicative second language programs can improve learners' use of particular grammatical features. The results also show, however, that the effects of instruction are not always long-lasting. For example, in the intensive ESL studies, the positive effects of form-focused instruction on adverb placement had disappeared a year later. Yet, the positive effects of this type of instruction and corrective feedback for questions were maintained in the long-term follow-up testing. These results might be explained in terms of the frequency of use of the two linguistic structures in regular classroom input after the experimental treatment had ended—question forms occurred much more frequently. Thus, opportunities for continued use may have contributed to the continued improvement in the learners' use of questions over time. Evidence from classroom observations suggests that students did not receive any continued exposure to adverbs in classroom materials and activities once the experimental period was over, and it is not surprising that they failed to maintain the improved performance levels.

These results of the research into form-focused instruction within communicative language teaching also suggest that form-focused instruction may be more successful with some language features than with others. The successful learning of the *tu/vous* distinction in Lyster's study could be due to the fact that learning *tu* and *vous* is essentially a matter of learning two important vocabulary items and thus may have been less difficult to learn than more complex syntactic features. For example, Harley found that instructed learners continued to experience difficulty with the *passé composé/imparfait* contrast where the form–meaning relationship is more complex.

The implications of classroom research for teaching

Many questions have been raised by the research which has been done to test the hypotheses which the different proposals represent. Although there is still much work to do, it is possible to speculate on the 'strongest contenders' on the basis of the classroom research findings so far.

One thing is clear. Some exceptionally gifted learners will succeed in second language learning regardless of the method. In the schools of the world, the most widely applied method is no doubt the grammar translation method. Most of us have met individuals whose mastery of a foreign language is based largely on their experience in such classes. Similarly, audiolingual classes produced some highly proficient second language learners. However, we also know—from personal experience and research findings—that these methods, when experienced in the absence of opportunities to use the language for meaningful interaction, leave many learners frustrated and unable to participate in ordinary conversations. No doubt grammar translation and audiolingual approaches will continue to be used, but the evidence suggests that 'Get it right from the beginning' does not correspond to the way most successful second language learners have acquired their proficiency. On the other hand, in throwing out contrastive analysis, feedback on error, and metalinguistic explanations and guidance, the 'communicative revolution' may have gone too far.

There is increasing evidence that learners continue to have difficulty with basic structures of the language in programs which offer no form-focused instruction. This calls into question the 'Just listen . . . and read' proposal, which in its strongest form not only claims no benefit from form-focused instruction and correction, but suggests that such form focus can actually interfere with second language development. There is good evidence that learners make considerable progress in both comprehension and production in strictly comprehension-based programs. However, we do not find support for the argument that if second language learners are simply exposed to comprehensible input, language acquisition will take care of itself.

There are similar problems with the 'Say what you mean and mean what you say' proposal. As noted earlier in this chapter, opportunities for learners to engage in conversational interactions in group and paired activities can lead to increased fluency and the ability to manage conversations in a second language. However, the research also shows that learners in programs based on the 'Say what you mean and mean what you say' proposal, where there is no guided focus on form, continue to have difficulty with accuracy as well. Because this approach emphasizes meaning and attempts to simulate 'natural' communication in conversational interaction, the students' focus is naturally on *what* they say, not *how* to say it. This can result in a situation where learners provide each other with input which is often incorrect and incomplete. Furthermore, when feedback on error takes the form of recasts or repetitions only, it may be interpreted by the learners as a continuation of the conversation. Thus, programs based on the 'Say what you mean and mean what you say' approach are incomplete in that learners' gains in fluency and conversational skills may not be matched by their development of accuracy.

It is important to emphasize that the evidence to support a role for form-focused instruction and corrective feedback does not suggest a return to the 'Get it right from the beginning' approach. Research has demonstrated that learners *do* benefit considerably from communicative interaction and instruction which is meaning-based. The results of research into French immersion, content-based courses, and intensive ESL research are strong indicators that learners develop higher levels of fluency through primarily meaning-based instruction than through rigidly grammar-based instruction. The problem remains, however, that certain aspects of linguistic knowledge and performance are not fully developed in such programs.

Unfortunately, research investigating the 'Teach what is teachable' proposal is not yet at a point where it is possible to say to teachers: 'Here is a list of linguistic features and the order in which they will be acquired. You should teach them in this order.' The number of features which researchers have investigated in experimental studies within this framework is simply far too small. Furthermore, there has been no strong evidence that teaching according to the developmental sequences will improve the long-term results in language learning. However, this proposal does serve to help teachers set realistic expectations about the ways in which learners' interlanguage may change in response to instruction.

In the 'Get it right in the end' position, the emphasis is primarily on meaning, but those who hold this position argue that there is a role for form-focused instruction and correction. The research relevant to this proposal has shown that second language learners benefit from form-focused instruction which is provided within communicative contexts. The challenge is to find the balance between meaning-based and form-focused activities. The right balance is likely to be different according to the characteristics of the learners. The learners' age, metalinguistic sophistication, motivation, goals, and the similarity of the target language to a language already known need to be taken into account when decisions are made about the amount and type of form-focus to offer.

Birgit Harley (1993) has offered some suggestions about how to identify features for form focus. In her review of research in French immersion programs, she argues that form-focused instruction is needed for those features which: (a) differ in non-obvious or unexpected ways from the learners' first language; (b) are irregular, infrequent, or lack perceptual salience in the second language input; and (c) do not carry a heavy communicative load. The features she targets as prime candidates for form-focused instruction in French second language instruction are:

- gender distinctions
- lexical distinctions across first language and second language (for example, mistaking 'temps' for time, instead of 'l'heure' as in 'Savez-vous le temps [weather]?' instead of 'Savez-vous l'heure?')
- distinctions in the use of 'avoir' and 'être'
- various features of the verb system such as the use of the *imparfait*, conditional, and third person plural agreement in the present tense
- distinctions between *tu* and *vous*.

On the other hand, Harley claims many other features can be learned *without* form-focused instruction. These include: high-frequency vocabulary items, features which are phonologically salient, and grammatical patterns which are congruent with the learners' first language.

The results from research in intensive ESL programs point to the need for form-focused instruction when features in the second language differ from the learners' first language in subtle ways, particularly when the information about these differences is not available in the regularly occurring input (for example, adverb placement). At times, it may be necessary to provide explicit information about how learners' first languages contrast with the target language. This may be particularly important in classrooms where all the students share the same first language. This information need not be prolonged or complicated, and can be quickly and easily incorporated into a lesson in which the primary focus is on meaning and communication. The research on corrective feedback in French immersion discussed in Chapter 5 by Lyster and Ranta (see pages 103–6), and explicit feedback and instruction in content-based ESL (study 25, page 148) provides particularly strong support for such a recommendation.

Summary

Classroom data from a number of studies offer support for the view that form-focused instruction and corrective feedback provided within the context of communicative programs are more effective in promoting second language learning than programs which are limited to a virtually exclusive emphasis either on accuracy or on fluency. Thus, we would argue that second language teachers can (and should) provide guided, form-based instruction and corrective feedback in certain circumstances. For example, teachers should not hesitate to correct persistent errors which learners seem not to notice without focused attention. Teachers should also be especially aware of errors that the majority of learners in a class are making when they share the same first language background, and they should not hesitate to point out how a particular structure in a learner's first language differs from the target language. Teachers might also try to become more aware of those structures which they sense are just beginning to emerge in the second language development of their students and provide some guided instruction in the use of these forms. It may be useful to encourage learners to take part in the process by creating activities which draw their attention to the forms they use in communicative activities, by developing contexts in which they can provide each other with feedback, and by encouraging them to ask questions about language forms.

Decisions about when and how to provide form focus must take into account differences in learner characteristics, of course. Quite different approaches would be appropriate for, say, trained linguists learning a fourth or fifth language, young children beginning their schooling in a second language environment, immigrants who cannot read and write their own language, and adolescents studying a foreign language for a few hours a week at school.

It could be argued that many teachers are quite aware of the need to balance form-focus and meaning-focus, and that recommendations based on research may simply mean that sla research has confirmed current classroom practice. Although this may be true to some extent, it is hardly the case that all teachers have a clear sense of how best to accomplish their goal. It is not always easy to step back from familiar practices and say, 'I wonder if this is really the most effective way to go about this?' Furthermore, many teachers are reluctant to try out classroom practices which go against the prevailing trends among their colleagues or in their educational contexts. Many teachers still work in environments where there is an emphasis on accuracy which virtually excludes spontaneous language use in the classroom. At the same time, the introduction of communicative language teaching methods has sometimes resulted in a complete rejection of attention to form and error correction in second language teaching. But it is not necessary to choose between form-based and meaning-based instruction. Rather, the challenge is to find the best balance of these two orientations. Which features of language will respond best to form-focused instruction, and which will be acquired without explicit focus if learners have adequate exposure to the language? Which learners will respond well to metalinguistic information and which will require some other way of focusing attention on language form? When should corrective feedback be offered and when should learners be allowed to focus their attention on the content of their utterances? Continued classroom-centred research, including the informal research which teachers can do in their own classrooms, should provide us with further insights into these and other important issues in second language teaching and learning.

Sources and suggestions for further reading

Overviews of language teaching approaches

Brown, H. D. 1994. *Teaching by Principles: An Interactive Approach to Language Pedagogy*. Englewood Cliffs, N.J.: Prentice-Hall Regents.

Larsen-Freeman, D. 2000. *Techniques and Principles in Language Teaching*. (Second Edition). Oxford: Oxford University Press.

Richards, J. and T. Rodgers. 1986. *Approaches and Methods in Language Teaching*. Cambridge: Cambridge University Press.

Get it right from the beginning

Hammerly, H. 1987. 'The immersion approach: litmus test of second-language acquisition through classroom communication.' *Modern Language Journal* 71/4: 395–401.

Higgs, T. V. and **R. Clifford.** 1982. 'The push toward communication' in T. V. Higgs (ed.): *Curriculum, Competence, and the Foreign Language Teacher.* Skokie, Ill.: National Textbook Co. pp. 57–79.

Lado, R. 1964. *Language Teaching: A Scientific Approach.* New York: McGraw-Hill.

Study 1: Audiolingual pattern drill

Lightbown, P. M. 1983. 'Acquiring English L2 in Quebec classrooms' in S. Felix and H. Wode (eds.): *Language Development at the Crossroads.* Tübingen: Gunter Narr. pp. 151–75.

Lightbown, P. M. 1987. 'Classroom language as input to second language acquisition' in C. Pfaff (ed.): *First and Second Language Acquisition Processes.* Cambridge, Mass.: Newbury House. pp. 169–87.

Study 2: Grammar plus communicative practice

Savignon, S. 1972. *Communicative Competence: An Experiment in Foreign-language Teaching.* Philadelphia, Pa.: Center for Curriculum Development.

Study 3: Grammar plus communicative practice

Montgomery, C. and **M. Eisenstein.** 1985. 'Reality revisited: An experimental communicative course in ESL.' *TESOL Quarterly* 19/2: 317–34.

Say what you mean and mean what you say

Gass, S. and **E. Varonis.** 1985. 'Task variation and nonnative/nonnative negotiation of meaning' in S. Gass and C. Madden (eds.): *Input in Second Language Acquisition.* Rowley, Mass.: Newbury House. pp. 149–61.

Gass, S. and **E. Varonis.** 1994. 'Input, interaction and second language production.' *Studies in Second Language Acquisition* 16/3: 283–302.

Gass, S., A. Mackey, and **T. Pica.** 1998. 'The role of input and interaction in second language acquisition: An introduction.' *Modern Language Journal* 82/3: 299–307.

Study 4: Group work and learner language

Long, M. H., L. Adams, M. McLean, and **F. Castanos.** 1976. 'Doing things with words: verbal interaction in lockstep and small group classroom situations' in J. Faneslow and R. Crymes (eds.): *On TESOL '76.* Washington, D.C.: TESOL. pp. 137–53.

Study 5: Learners talking to learners

Porter, P. 1986. 'How learners talk to each other: Input and interaction in task-centred discussions' in R. Day (ed.): *Talking to Learn: Conversation in Second Language Acquisition.* Rowley Mass.: Newbury House, pp. 200–22.

Long, M. H. and **P. Porter.** 1985. 'Group work, interlanguage talk, and second language acquisition.' *TESOL Quarterly* 19/2: 207–28.

Study 6: Learner language and proficiency level

Yule, G. and **D. Macdonald.** 1990. 'Resolving referential conflicts in L2 interaction: The effect of proficiency and interactive role.' *Language Learning* 40/4: 539–56.

Study 7: Interaction and comprehensibility

Pica, T., R. Young, and **C. Doughty.** 1987. 'The impact of interaction on comprehension.' *TESOL Quarterly* 21/4: 737–59.

Study 8: Interaction and second language development

Mackey, A. 1999. 'Input, interaction and second language development: An empirical study of question formation in ESL.' *Studies in Second Language Acquisition* 21/4, 557–87.

Study 9: Interaction with recasts

Mackey, A. and **J. Philp.** 1998. 'Conversational interaction and second language development: Recasts, responses and Red Herrings.' *Modern Language Journal* 82/3: 338–56.

Just listen . . . and read

Krashen, S. 1982. *Principles and Practice in Second Language Acquisition.* Oxford: Pergamon.

Krashen, S. 1985. *The Input Hypothesis: Issues and Implications.* London: Longman.

Study 10: Comprehension-based instruction for children

Lightbown, P. M. 1992. 'Can they do it themselves? A comprehension-based ESL course for young children' in R. Courchêne, J. Glidden, J. St John, and C. Thérein (eds.): *Comprehension-based Second Language Teaching/L'Enseignement des langues secondes axé sur la compréhension*. Ottawa: University of Ottawa Press. pp. 353–70.

Study 11: Total physical response

Asher, J. 1972. 'Children's first language as a model for second language learning.' *Modern Language Journal* 56/3: 133–9.

Study 12: French immersion programs in Canada

Harley, B. and **M. Swain.** 1984. 'The interlanguage of immersion students and its implications for second language teaching' in A. Davies, C. Criper, and A. Howatt (eds.): *Interlanguage*. Edinburgh: Edinburgh University Press. pp. 291–311.

Swain, M. 1985. 'Communicative competence: some roles of comprehensible input and comprehensible output in its development' in S. Gass and C. Madden (eds.): *Input in Second Language Acquisition*. Rowley, Mass.: Newbury House, pp. 235–53.

Swain, M. 1988. 'Manipulating and complementing content teaching to maximize second language learning.' *TESL Canada Journal* 6/1: 68–83.

Study 13: Input flood

Trahey, M. and **L. White.** 1993 'Positive evidence and preemption in the second language classroom.' *Studies in Second Language Acquisition* 15/2: 181–204.

White, L. 1987. 'Against comprehensible input: the input hypothesis and the development of L2 competence.' *Applied Linguistics* 8/2: 95–100.

Study 14: Enhanced input

Sharwood Smith, M. 1993. 'Input enhancement in instructed SLA: Theoretical bases.' *Studies in Second Language Acquisition* 15/2: 165–79.

White, J. 1998. 'Getting the learners' attention: A typographical input enhancement study' in C. Doughty and J. Williams (eds.): *Focus on Form in Classroom SLA*. Cambridge: Cambridge University Press, pp. 85–113.

Study 15: Input processing

VanPatten, B. and **T. Cadierno.** 1993. 'Explicit instruction and input processing.' *Studies in Second Language Acquisition* 15/2: 225–41.

VanPatten, B. and C. Sanz. 1995. 'From input to output: Processing instruction and communicative tasks' in F. Eckman, D. Highland, P. Lee, J. Mileham, and R. Weber (eds.): *Second Language Acquisition: Theory and Pedagogy.* Mahwah, N.J.: Lawrence Erlbaum Associates, pp. 169–85.

Teach what is teachable

Eckman, F., L. Bell, and D Nelson. 1988. 'On the generalization of relative clause instruction in the acquisition of English as a second language.' *Applied Linguistics* 9/1: 1–20.

Hamilton, R. 1994. 'Is implicational generalization unidirectional and maximal? Evidence from relativization instruction in a second language.' *Language Learning* 44/1: 123–57.

Lightbown, P. M. 1998. 'The importance of timing in focus on form' in C. Doughty and J. Williams (eds.): *Focus on Form in Classroom SLA.* Cambridge: Cambridge University Press, pp. 177–96.

Pienemann, M. 1985. 'Learnability and syllabus construction' in K. Hyltenstam and M. Pienemann (eds.): *Modelling and Assessing Second Language Acquisition.* Clevedon, UK: Multilingual Matters. pp. 23–75.

Pienemann, M., M. Johnston, and G. Brindley. 1988. 'Constructing an acquisition-based procedure for second language assessment.' *Studies in Second Language Acquisition* 10/2: 217–43.

Study 16: Ready to learn

Pienemann, M. 1988. 'Determining the influence of instruction on L2 speech processing.' *AILA Review* 5/1: 40–72.

Study 17: Teaching when the time is right

Doughty, C. 1991. 'Second language instruction does make a difference: Evidence from an empirical study of SL relativization.' *Studies in Second Language Acquisition* 13/4: 431–69.

Study 18: Can question forms be taught?

Ellis, R. 1984. 'Can syntax be taught?' *Applied Linguistics* 5/2: 138–55.

Study 19: Developmental stage and the influence of L1

Spada, N. and P. M. Lightbown. 1999. 'Instruction, L1 influence and developmental readiness in second language acquisition.' *Modern Language Review* 83/1.

Get it right in the end

Doughty, C. and **J. Williams** (eds.). 1998. *Focus on Form in Classroom Second Language Acquisition*. Cambridge: Cambridge University Press.

Harley, B. 1993. 'Instructional strategies and SLA in early French immersion.' *Studies in Second Language Acquisition* 15/2: 245–59.

Lightbown, P. M. 1991. 'What have we here? Some observations on the role of instruction in second language acquisition' in R. Phillipson, E. Kellerman, L. Selinker, M. Sharwood Smith, and M. Swain (eds.): *Foreign/Second Language Pedagogy Research: A Commemorative Volume for Claus Færch*. Clevedon, UK: Multilingual Matters, pp. 197–212.

Long, M. H. 1991. 'Focus on form: a design feature in language teaching methodology' in K. de Bot, D. Coste, R. Ginsberg, and C. Kramsch (eds.): *Foreign Language Research in Cross-cultural Perspective*. Amsterdam: John Benjamins. pp. 39–52.

Long, M.H. and **G. Crookes.** 1992. 'Three approaches to task-based syllabus design.' *TESOL Quarterly* 26/1: 27–56.

Lyster, R. 1998. 'Recasts, repetition and ambiguity in L2 classroom discourse.' *Studies in Second Language Acquisition* 20/1: 51–81.

Rutherford, W. 1987. 'The meaning of grammatical consciousness-raising.' *World Englishes* 6/3: 209–16.

Sharwood Smith, M. 1991. 'Speaking to many minds: on the relevance of different types of language information for the L2 learner.' *Second Language Research* 7/2: 118–32.

White, L. 1987. 'Against comprehensible input: the input hypothesis and the development of second-language competence.' *Applied Linguistics* 8/2: 95–110.

Study 20: Attention to form in communicative ESL

Spada, N. 1987. 'Relationships between instructional differences and learning outcomes: a process-product study of communicative language teaching.' *Applied Linguistics* 8/2: 137–61.

Study 21: Form-focus experiments in ESL

Lightbown, P. M. and **N. Spada.** 1994. 'An innovative program for primary ESL in Quebec.' *TESOL Quarterly* 28/3: 563–79.

Spada, N. and **P. M. Lightbown.** 1993. 'Instruction and the development of questions in L2 classrooms.' *Studies in Second Language Acquisition* 15/2: 205–24.

White, L. 1991. 'Adverb placement in second language acquisition: some effects of positive and negative evidence in the classroom.' *Second Language Research* 7/2: 133–61.

White, L., N. Spada, P. M. Lightbown, and L. Ranta. 1991. 'Input enhancement and syntactic accuracy in L2 acquisition.' *Applied Linguistics* 12/4: 416–32.

Study 22: Focusing on past tense forms in French immersion

Harley, B. 1989. 'Functional grammar in French immersion: A classroom experiment.' *Applied Linguistics* 10/3: 331–59.

Study 23: Focusing on the conditional in French immersion

Day, E. and S. Shapson. 1991. 'Integrating formal and functional approaches to language teaching in French immersion: An experimental approach.' *Language Learning* 41/1: 25–58.

Study 24: Focusing on sociolinguistic forms in French immersion

Lyster, R. 1994. 'The effect of functional-analytic teaching on aspects of French immersion students' sociolinguistic competence.' *Applied Linguistics* 15/3: 263–87.

Study 25: Focusing on verb form in content-based science classrooms

Doughty, C. and E. Varela. 1997. 'Communicative focus on form' in C. Doughty and J. Williams (eds.): *Focus on Form in Classroom SLA*. Cambridge: Cambridge University Press, pp. 114–38.

Study 26: Focusing on form in learner–learner interaction

Kowal, M. and M. Swain. 1994. 'Using collaborative language production tasks to promote students' language awareness.' *Language Awareness* 3/2: 73–91.

Wajnryb, R. 1990. *Grammar Dictation*. Oxford: Oxford University Press.

7 POPULAR IDEAS ABOUT LANGUAGE LEARNING: FACTS AND OPINIONS

In the Introduction, we presented a number of commonly expressed opinions about how languages are learned. We asked you to indicate how strongly you agreed with these opinions. Now that you have read about some of the theory and research in second language acquisition, take another look at those ideas. Have you changed your mind about the importance of imitation or group-work, or whether starting second language instruction early is really the best approach? Or do you feel that your views about SLA have only been confirmed by the discussion in the preceding chapters?

To conclude this introduction to SLA research, here are our own responses to these popular ideas about language learning.

1 Languages are learned mainly through imitation

It is difficult to find support for the argument that languages are learned mainly through imitation. For one thing, learners produce many novel sentences that they could not have heard before. These sentences are based on the learners' developing understanding of how the language system works. This is particularly evident with children who say things like: 'I'm hiccing up and I can't stop' and 'It was upside down but I turned it upside right' or with second language learners who say 'The cowboy rided into town' or 'The man that I spoke to him is angry.' These examples and many others provide evidence that language learners do not simply internalize a great list of imitated and memorized sentences.

This does not mean, however, that imitation has no role to play in language learning. Some children imitate a great deal as they acquire their first language. Yet their language does not develop faster or better than that of children who rarely imitate. Furthermore, children do not imitate everything they hear, but often selectively imitate certain words or structures which they are in the process of learning.

Second language learners also produce many sentences that they could not have heard. In this way, they are like children learning their first language. Some second language learners may find that they benefit from opportunities to imitate samples of the new language, and imitation is clearly important in developing proficiency in pronunciation and intonation. For some advanced learners who are determined to improve their pronunciation, careful listening and imitation in a language laboratory can be very valuable. But for beginning learners, the slavish imitation and rote memorization that characterized audiolingual language approaches to language teaching led many learners to a dead end. They could recite bits of perfectly accurate language, but the lack of practice in struggling to understand and make themselves understood in genuinely meaningful interaction left many learners with little more than a collection of sentences, waiting for the moment when those sentences would be useful!

2 *Parents usually correct young children when they make grammatical errors*

There is considerable variation in the extent to which parents correct their children's speech. The variation is based partly on the children's age. When children are very young pre-schoolers, parents rarely comment on grammatical errors although they may correct lapses in politeness or the choice of a word that doesn't make sense. As children reach school age, parents often correct the kinds of non-standard speech that they hope their children will outgrow, for example, 'Me and Fred are going outside now.' The parents' own sociolinguistic background is also a source of variation in the amount and kind of correction they engage in. Some parents hear nothing wrong in the grammar of 'That's the boy who I gave my books to' while others will insist on 'to whom'.

Nevertheless, extensive observations of parents and children show that, as a rule, parents tend to focus on meaning rather than form when they correct children's speech. Thus, they may correct an incorrect word choice, an incorrect statement of the facts, or a rude remark, but they either do not notice or do not react to errors which do not interfere with successful communication. What this tells us is that children cannot depend on consistent corrective feedback in order to learn the basic structure (the word order, the grammatical morphemes, the intonation patterns) of their language. Fortunately, they appear to be able to acquire the adult form of the language with little or no explicit feedback.

The case for second language learners is more complex. While it is clear that older children and adults can acquire a great deal of language without any formal instruction, the evidence suggests that, without corrective feedback and guidance, second language learners may persist in using certain ungrammatical forms for years.

3 People with high IQs are good language learners

The kind of intelligence which is measured by IQ tests is a good predictor for success in classrooms where the emphasis is on learning *about* the language (for example, grammar rules and vocabulary items). In addition, people who do well on IQ tests may do well on other kinds of tests as well. However, in natural language learning settings and in classrooms where language acquisition through interactive language use is emphasized, research has shown that learners with a wide variety of intellectual abilities can be successful language learners. This is especially true if the skills which are assessed are oral communication skills rather than metalinguistic knowledge.

4 The most important factor in second language acquisition success is motivation

Everyone agrees that learners who want to learn tend to do better than those who don't. But we must guard against too strong an interpretation of this. Sometimes, even highly motivated learners encounter great difficulties in improving their mastery of the language. We know, for example, that learners who begin learning a second language as adults rarely achieve the fluency and accuracy that children do in first language acquisition. This failure to achieve native-like ability cannot be taken as evidence that adult second language learners are not motivated to learn the language. We also know that in a group of highly motivated second language learners, there are always those who are more successful than others. This is sometimes due to differences in language learning aptitude and in how the instruction interacts with individual learners' styles and preferences for learning.

Clearly, teachers have no influence over a learner's intrinsic motivation for learning a second language. Learners come into our classrooms from different backgrounds and life experiences, all of which have contributed to their attitudes toward and motivation to learn the target language. The principal way that teachers can influence learners' motivation is by making the classroom a supportive environment in which students are stimulated, engaged in activities which are appropriate to their age, interests and cultural backgrounds, and, most importantly, where students can experience success. This in turn can contribute to positive motivation, leading to still greater success.

5 The earlier a second language is introduced in school programs, the greater the likelihood of success in learning

The decision about when to introduce second or foreign language instruction must depend on the objectives of the language program in the particular social context of the school. When the objective is native-like performance in the second language, then it may be desirable to begin exposure to the language as early as possible. The research evidence is fairly strong that only those who begin second language learning at an early age will eventually be indistinguishable from native speakers.

However, even in cases where such high levels of skill are targeted, it is important to recognize certain disadvantages of an early start, especially when an early start in second language means that children have little opportunity to continue to develop their knowledge of their first language. Subtractive bilingualism may have lasting negative consequences. For children from minority-language backgrounds, programs promoting the development of the first language at home and at school may be more important for long-term success in the second language than an early start in the second language itself. Research shows that a good foundation in the child's first language, including the development of literacy, is a sound base to build on. Children who can begin their schooling in a language they already know will have more self-confidence, will be able to learn more effectively in the early school years, and will not lose valuable time in a period of limbo during which they struggle just to understand what is happening in the classroom.

Clearly, for many children, there is no opportunity to have their early schooling in their first language. They are members of a small minority group where it is not practical for schools to offer them an educational program in their first language, or they live in jurisdictions where legislation has mandated a single language of education for all children, regardless of their background. For these children, it is crucial to have sensitive educators who respect the children's difficulty, who encourage parents to maintain the home language, and who understand that second language learning takes time and effort.

For foreign language instruction or for second language instruction where the level of proficiency which is targeted is not native-like performance by all students, the situation is quite different. When the goal of the educational program is basic communicative skill for all students, and where there is a strong commitment to maintaining and developing the child's first language, it can be more efficient to begin second language teaching later. Older children (for example, 10-year olds) are able to catch up very quickly on those who began earlier (for example, at 6 or 7 years old) in programs offering only a few hours a week of instruction. This is especially true if the foreign language course includes a period of more intensive exposure to the new language. All school programs should be based on realistic estimates of how long it takes to learn a second language. One or two hours a week – even for seven or eight years – will not produce very advanced second language speakers. This 'drip-feed' approach often leads to frustration as learners feel that they have been studying 'for years' without making much progress. Sadly, they are sometimes right about this.

6 *Most of the mistakes which second language learners make are due to interference from their first language*

The transfer of patterns from the native language is undoubtedly one of the major sources of errors in learner language. However, there are other causes for errors too, one of which is overgeneralization of target-language rules. For example, research has shown that second language learners from different first-language backgrounds often make the same kinds of errors when learning a particular second language. In such cases, second-language errors are evidence of the learners' efforts to discover the structure of the target language itself rather than attempts to transfer patterns from their first language. Interestingly, some of these errors are remarkably similar to the kinds of errors made by first language learners.

These observations are a strong indication that second language learning is not simply a process of putting second-language words into first-language sentences. Research has also shown that aspects of the second language which are different from the first language will not necessarily be acquired later or with more difficulty than those aspects which are similar.

On the other hand, when errors are caused by the overextension of some partial similarity between the first and second languages, these errors may be difficult to overcome. This may be particularly problematic if learners are frequently in contact with other learners who make the same errors.

7 *Teachers should present grammatical rules one at a time, and learners should practise examples of each one before going on to another*

Language learning is not simply linear in its development. Learners may use a particular form accurately at stage x (suggesting that they have learned that form), fail to produce that form at stage y, and produce it accurately again at stage z. The decline in accuracy may show that learners are incorporating new information about the language into their own internal system of rules. An example of this would be when learners who have learned the past tense form 'went' as a memorized 'chunk' learn to use the regular *-ed* inflection for past tense marking. At this point, they stop using 'went'and produce 'goed'. Once learners become aware of the exceptions to the *-ed* past tense rule, they begin to use 'went'correctly again. This provides evidence that language development is not just adding rule after rule, but integrating new rules into an existing system of rules, readjusting and restructuring until all the pieces fit.

Some structure-based approaches to teaching are based on the false assumption that second language development is linear. This can be seen in the organization of textbooks which introduce a particular language feature in the first unit and reinforce it in several subsequent units before moving onto the next feature. This isolated presentation and practice of one structure at a time does not provide learners with an opportunity to discover how different language features compare and contrast in normal language use.

8 Teachers should teach simple language structures before complex ones

Research has shown that no matter how language is presented to learners, certain structures are acquired before others. This suggests that it is neither necessary nor desirable to restrict learners' exposure to certain linguistic structures which are perceived in linguistic terms to be 'simple' – particularly when this involves the isolated presentation, ordering, and practice of 'simple' to 'complex' features.

At the same time, there is no doubt that second language learners benefit from the efforts of native speakers and fluent bilinguals to modify their speech to help second language learners understand. This modified speech contains a variety of linguistic structures, but omits complex forms. It also includes a range of conversational adjustments which enable second language learners to engage in interactions with native and more advanced speakers of the second language more easily. Teachers, like parents, appear to be able to increase the complexity of their language intuitively as the learner's proficiency increases.

Teachers must also be aware, however, that some linguistic forms are so rare in their everyday speech that learners have very little opportunity to hear, use, and learn them if the teacher does not make a point of providing them. These are not necessarily difficult or complex forms, however. As we saw in Chapter 6 (pages 131–2), in study 13 carried out in intensive communicative ESL classes in Quebec, teachers almost never used adverbs!

9 *Learners' errors should be corrected as soon as they are made in order to prevent the formation of bad habits*

Errors are a natural part of language learning. This is true of the development of a child's first language as well as of second language learning by children and adults. The errors reveal the patterns of learners' developing interlanguage systems – showing where they have overgeneralized a second language rule or where they have inappropriately transferred a first language rule to the second language.

When errors are persistent, especially when they are shared by almost all students in a class, it is useful to bring the problem to the learners' attention. This does not mean learners should be expected to adopt the correct form or structure immediately or consistently. If the error is based on a developmental pattern, the correction may only be useful when the learner is ready for it. It may thus require many repetitions.

Teachers have a responsibility to help learners do their best, and this sometimes means drawing their attention to persistent errors. Excessive feedback on error can have a negative effect on motivation, of course, and teachers must be sensitive to the way their students react to correction. The kind of correction which is offered will also vary according to the specific characteristics of the students. Children and adults with little education in their first language will not benefit greatly from sophisticated metalinguistic explanations, but university students who are advanced learners of the language may find such explanations of great value. Immediate reaction to errors in an oral communication setting may embarrass some students and discourage them from speaking, while for others, such correction is exactly what is needed to help them notice a persistent error at just the moment when it occurs. The research on corrective feedback does show that, in classrooms which are content based (for example, immersion classes), feedback which is given exclusively or principally in the form of conversational 'recasts' passes unnoticed. Learners may not recognize it as correction unless the teacher has a method of signalling to the student – through tone of voice, a gesture, or facial expression – which says to the student, 'I think I understand what you are saying and I'm telling you how you can say it better.'

10   *Teachers should use materials that expose students only to language structures which they have already been taught*

Such a procedure can provide comprehensible input of course, but—given a meaningful context—learners can comprehend the general meaning of many forms which they certainly have not 'mastered' and, indeed, may never have produced. Thus, restricting classroom second language materials to those which contain little or nothing which is new may have several negative consequences. There will undoubtedly be a loss of motivation if students are not sufficiently challenged. Students also need to deal with 'real' or 'authentic' material if they are eventually going to be prepared for language use outside the classroom. They do this first with the teacher's guidance and then independently. Restricting students to step-by-step exposure to the language extends their dependency.

When a particular form is introduced for the first time, or when the teacher feels there is a need for correction of a persistent problem, it is appropriate to use narrow-focus materials which isolate one element in a context where other things seem easy. But it would be a disservice to students to use such materials exclusively or even predominantly. We should remember that learners who successfully acquire English outside classrooms certainly are exposed to a variety of forms and structures which they have not mastered.

11   *When learners are allowed to interact freely (for example, in group or pair activities), they learn each others' mistakes*

There is good evidence that, if the tasks are well designed, learners working in groups get far more practice in speaking and participating in conversations in group work than they ever could in a teacher-centred class. Somewhat surprisingly, the research has also shown that learners do not produce any more errors in their speech when talking to learners at similar levels of proficiency than they do when speaking to learners at more advanced levels or to native speakers. This research also shows, however, that learners at similar levels cannot provide each other with information which would help to correct those errors. Some other studies show that tasks can be devised in such a way that learners working together can discover information or knowledge about the second language they didn't know they had. In order for this to happen, the tasks must be carefully planned and the learners must have access to the correct language forms they are trying to discover.

Group work is a valuable addition to the variety of activities which encourage and promote second language development. Used in combination with individual work and teacher-centred activities, it plays an important role in communicative language teaching.

12 *Students learn what they are taught*

Clearly, second language learners can only learn the language they are exposed to. But it is certainly not the case that students learn everything they are taught or that they eventually know only what they are taught. Some teaching methods typically give learners the opportunity to learn only a very restricted number of words and sentence types. Even when the language teaching method provides much richer language input, the fact that something is taught or made available in the input does not mean learners will acquire it right away. For example, some aspects of the second language develop according to 'natural' sequences of development and learners may be more likely to learn certain language features when they are developmentally 'ready'. Thus, attempts to teach aspects of language which are too far away from the learner's current stage of development will usually be frustrating.

Other aspects of language, however, for example, vocabulary, can be taught at any time, as long as the learners are interested in the opportunity to learn and the teaching methods are appropriate to the learner's age, interests, and learning styles. Fortunately, research has also shown that learners can learn a great deal that no-one ever teaches them. They are able to use their own internal learning mechanisms to discover many of the complex rules and relationships which underlie the language they wish to learn. Students, in this sense, may be said to learn much more than they are taught.

Conclusion

Knowing more about second language acquisition research will not tell you what to do in your classroom tomorrow morning. We hope, however, that this book has provided you with information which encourages you to reflect on your experience in teaching. We hope, in addition, that this reflection will contribute to a better understanding of your responsibilities as a teacher and those of your students as language learners.

As we have seen, language learning is affected by many factors. Among these are the personal characteristics of the learner, the structure of the native and target languages, opportunities for interaction with speakers of the target language, and access to correction and form-focused instruction. It is clear that teachers do not have control over all these factors. However, a better understanding of them will permit teachers and learners to make the most of the time they spend together in the twin processes of teaching and learning a second language.

GLOSSARY

We have included in this glossary only those items which have a special or technical meaning in second language acquisition research and second language teaching. The definitions are intended to reflect the terms *as we use them* in this book. Other writers may give different interpretations to some of them. As a rule, we have not included words for which definitions can readily be found in a dictionary (for example, interlocutor, empirical).

accuracy order: The relative accuracy of grammatical forms in learner language. For example, learners are often more accurate in using plural-*s* than in using possessive-*'s*. Some researchers have inferred that an accuracy order is equivalent to a sequence of acquisition.

American Sign Language (ASL): The gestural language used by many North Americans who are deaf or who interact with deaf persons. It is a true language, with complex rules of structure and a rich vocabulary, all expressed through motions of the hands and body.

audiolingual approach: Audiolingual teaching is based on the *behaviourist* theory of learning and on structural linguistics. This instructional approach emphasizes the formation of habits through the practice, memorization, and repetition of grammatical structures in isolation from each other and from contexts of meaningful use.

behaviourism: A psychological theory that all learning, whether verbal or non-verbal, takes place through the establishment of habits. According to this view, when learners imitate and repeat the language they hear in their surrounding environment and are positively reinforced for doing so, habit formation (or learning) occurs.

child-directed speech: The language which caretakers address to children. In some cases, this language is simpler than that which is addressed to adults and also may involve slower speech, more repetition, and a large number of questions.

classroom observation scheme: A tool (often in the form of a grid) which consists of a set of predetermined categories to describe teaching and learning behaviours.

cognitive maturity: The ability to engage in problem-solving, deduction, and complex memory tasks.

communicative competence: The ability to use language in a variety of settings, taking into account relationships between speakers and differences in situations. The term has sometimes been interpreted as the ability to convey messages in spite of a lack of grammatical accuracy.

communicative language teaching (CLT): CLT is based on the premise that successful language learning involves not only a knowledge of the structures and forms of a language, but also the functions and purposes that a language serves in different communicative settings. This approach to teaching emphasizes the communication of meaning over the practice and manipulation of grammatical forms.

competence: Chomsky used this term to refer to knowledge of language. This is contrasted with *performance*, which is the way a person actually uses language – whether for speaking, listening, or writing. Because we cannot observe competence directly, we have to infer its nature from performance.

comprehensible input: A term introduced by Stephen Krashen to refer to language which a learner can understand. The language may be comprehensible in part because of clues such as gestures, situations, or prior information.

comprehension-based instruction: A general term to describe a variety of second language programs in which the focus of instruction is on comprehension rather than production (for example, Total Physical Response).

connectionism: A theory which views language as a complex system of units which become interconnected in the mind as they are encountered together. The more often units are heard or seen together, the more likely it is that the presence of one will lead to the activation of the other.

content-based instruction: Second language programs in which lessons are organized around topics, themes, and/or subject-matter rather than language points (for example, French *immersion programs*).

Contrastive Analysis Hypothesis (CAH): The CAH predicts that where there are similarities between the first and second languages, the learner will acquire second language structures with ease; where there are differences, the learner will have difficulty.

control group: In experimental studies, a group of learners which, ideally, differs from the experimental group only in terms of the single factor which the researcher is investigating. Performance of the control group is used to show that the factor in question is the best (or only) explanation for changes in the experimental group.

corrective feedback: An indication to a learner that his or her use of the target language is incorrect. This includes a variety of responses that a language learner receives. Corrective feedback can be explicit (for example, 'No, you should say "goes", not "go"') or implicit (for example, 'Yes, he *goes* to school every day'), and may or may not include metalinguistic information (for example, 'Don't forget to make the verb agree with the subject').

correlation: A statistical procedure which compares the frequency or size of different factors in order to determine whether there is a relationship between the two. For example, if the students with the highest grades in French also spend the greatest number of hours doing their homework, this would be a positive correlation. It is important to keep in mind, however, that correlation does not imply that one of the variables causes the other. Successful learners may spend more time on homework because it gives them a feeling of accomplishment.

creative construction: A theory that second language acquisition is a process by which a learner constructs his/her own rule system (i.e. internal representations) for the language being learned. These internal representations are thought to develop slowly in the direction of the full second language system in predictable stages. Creative construction emphasizes the similarity of learners from different first language backgrounds and minimizes the importance of *transfer.*

Critical Period Hypothesis (*CPH*): The proposal that there is a specific and limited time period for language acquisition. There are two versions of the CPH. The *strong version* is that if a language is not learned by puberty the biological endowment which permits successful language acquisition will not be available. Thus the learner will have to use general learning mechanisms which are not designed for language acquisition and thus not as successful. The *weak version* is that, even though the same learning mechanisms are involved, second language learning will be more difficult and incomplete after puberty because most learners have neither the time nor the motivation to reach the high level of mastery which a child reaches.

cross-sectional study: A research method in which subjects at different ages and stages of development are studied. Inferences about sequences which would apply to the development of individual learners are sometimes drawn from cross-sectional studies. This contrasts with *longitudinal studies.*

descriptive study: Research which does not involve any manipulation, change, or intervention in the phenomenon being studied. The researcher's goal is to observe and record what is happening. This contrasts with *experimental study.*

developmental error: An error in learner language which does not result from first language influence but rather reflects the learner's gradual discovery of the second language system. These errors are often similar to those made by children learning the language as their mother tongue.

developmental features: Those aspects of a language which, according to Pienemann and his colleagues, develop in a particular sequence, regardless of input variation or instructional intervention.

developmental sequences: The order in which certain features of a language (for example, negation) are acquired in language learning. Also called *developmental stages.*

display question: A question to which the asker already knows the answer. Teachers often ask these questions (for example, 'What colour is your shirt?') not because they are genuinely interested in the answer, but rather, to get the learner to display his or her knowledge of the language.

enhanced input: Input which is altered in an effort to make it more salient to learners. It can be more or less explicit, ranging from explicit metalinguistic comments to typographical enhancement (*bold type* or *underlining*) or exaggerated stress in speaking.

ESL: English as a Second Language. This refers to the learning of English for use in a setting where English is the principal language (for example, immigrants learning English in Britain).

experimental study: Research which is designed to study the role or impact of one or more very specific variables. A strictly experimental study would have 'experimental' and 'control' groups which differ from each other only in the presence or absence of one variable. In educational research, it is often difficult to create all of the conditions which permit a study to be termed as a 'genuine' experimental study. In this book, the term is used in a non-technical sense to refer to research in which an attempt has been made to investigate a single variable in an educational setting.

field independent/field dependent: This distinction has been used to describe people who differ in their tendency to see the 'trees in the forest'. That is, some people (called 'field independent') are very quick to pick out the hidden figures in a complicated drawing. Others (called 'field dependent') are more inclined to see the whole drawing and have difficulty separating it into parts.

first language (mother tongue, native language, L1): The language first learned. Many children learn more than one language from birth and may be said to have more than one mother tongue. The abbreviation L1 is often used.

foreigner talk: The modified or simplified language which some native speakers address to second language learners. A special category of foreigner talk is *teacher talk.*

foreign language learning: This refers to the learning of a second (or third, or fourth) language in a context where the target language is not widely used in the community (for example, learning French in China). This is often contrasted with second language learning, i.e. where the language being learned is used in the community (for example, learning Italian in Florence).

formal language learning setting: A setting in which second language learners receive instruction and opportunities to practise. In this context, efforts are often made to develop the learner's awareness of how the language system works. Typically, this type of learning takes place in the classroom.

form-focused instruction: Instruction which draws attention to the forms and structures of the language within the context of communicative interaction. This may be done by giving metalinguistic information, simply highlighting the form in question, or by providing *corrective feedback*.

formulaic patterns or routines: These are expressions which are learned as unanalysed wholes of 'chunks' (for example, 'How old are you?').

fossilization: Interlanguage patterns which seem not to change, even after extended exposure to or instruction in the target language. The term may also be used to refer to errors which occur, somewhat unexpectedly, in the second language performance of proficient speakers when they are tired or under pressure.

genuine question: In contrast to *display questions*, genuine questions are asked when there is a focus on information: the asker does not know the answer in advance (for example, 'What did you do at the weekend?').

grammar translation: An approach to second language teaching which is characterized by the explicit instruction of grammatical rules and language analysis through the use of translation.

grammatical morphemes: Morphemes are the smallest units of language that carry meaning. A simple word is a morpheme (for example, 'book') but when we talk about 'grammatical morphemes' we are usually referring to smaller units which are added to words to alter their meaning (for example, the *-s* in books to indicate plural) or function words (for example, 'the') which are ordinarily attached to another word.

immersion program: An educational program in which a second language is taught via *content-based instruction*. That is, students study subjects such as mathematics and social studies in their second language. In these programs, the emphasis is on subject matter learning, and little time is spent focusing on the formal aspects of the second language. Typically, students in immersion programs all share the same first language.

informal language learning setting: A setting in which the second language is not taught, but rather, is learned naturally, i.e. 'on the job' or 'in the streets', through informal conversations and interactions with native speakers of the language being learned.

information processing: This psychological theory compares the human brain to a computer. It includes the idea that the brain has a very large capacity to store information in the long term, but a more limited capacity for information which requires our attention. After a certain amount of practice, things which at first required attention become automatic, leaving more attention available for focus on something else.

innatism: A theory that human beings are born with some basic knowledge about languages in general that makes it possible to learn the specific language of the environment.

input: The language which the learner is exposed to (either written or spoken) in the environment.

instrumental motivation: See *integrative motivation*.

integrative motivation/instrumental motivation: This distinction contrasts motivation for second language learning which is based on a desire to know more about the culture and community of the target language group and even a desire to be more like members of that group (integrative motivation) with motivation which is more practical, such as the need to learn the language in order to get a better job (instrumental motivation).

interactionism: A theory that language acquisition is based both on learners' innate abilities and on opportunities to engage in conversations, often those in which other speakers modify their speech to match the learners' communication requirements. The innate abilities are not seen as being specific to language or language acquisition.

interlanguage: The learner's developing second language knowledge. It may have characteristics of the learner's first language, characteristics of the second language, and some characteristics which seem to be very general and tend to occur in all or most interlanguage systems. Interlanguages are systematic, but they are also dynamic, continually evolving as learners receive more input and revise their hypotheses about the second language.

judgements of grammaticality: Responses to the question 'Is this a correct [or acceptable] sentence of English [or another language]?' In answering such questions, we are asked to focus on the form (grammar) of the sentence rather than on its meaning.

L1: See *first language*.

L2: See *second language* and *target language*.

language acquisition: This term is most often used interchangeably with *language learning*. However, for some researchers, most notably Stephen Krashen, acquisition is contrasted with learning. According to Krashen, acquisition represents 'unconscious' learning, which takes place when attention is focused on meaning rather than language form.

language acquisition device (LAD): A metaphor for the innate knowledge of the 'universal' principles common to all human languages. The presence of this knowledge permits children to discover the structure of a given language on the basis of a relatively small amount of input.

language learning: In this book, this term is a general one which simply refers to a learner's developing knowledge of the target language. In Stephen Krashen's terms, however, 'learning' is contrasted with 'acquisition', and is described as a 'conscious' process which occurs when the learner's objective is to learn about the language itself, rather than to understand messages which are conveyed through the language.

longitudinal study: A study in which the same learners are studied over a period of time. This contrasts with a *cross-sectional study.*

meaning-based instruction: See *communicative language teaching.*

metalinguistic awareness: The ability to treat language as an object, for example, being able to define a word, or to say what sounds make up that word.

modified input: Adapted speech which adults use to address children and native speakers use to address language learners so that the learner will be able to understand. Examples of modified input include shorter, simpler sentences, slower rate of speech, and basic vocabulary.

modified interaction: Adapted conversation patterns which proficient speakers use in addressing language learners so that the learner will be able to understand. Examples of interactional modifications include comprehension checks, clarification requests, and self-repetitions.

morpheme: See *grammatical morpheme.*

native-like: The ability to comprehend and produce a second language at a level of performance which is hardly distinguishable from that of a *native speaker.*

native speaker: A person who has learned a language from an early age and who has full mastery of that language. Native speakers may differ in terms of vocabulary and stylistic aspects of language use, but they tend to agree on the basic grammar of the language.

natural order: See *developmental sequences.*

negotiation of meaning: Interaction between speakers who make adjustments to their speech and use other techniques in order to facilitate communication. See also *modified interaction.*

obligatory contexts: Places in a sentence where a particular grammatical form is required if the sentence is to be correct. For example, in the sentence 'Yesterday, my brother rent a car', the speaker has created an obligatory context for the past tense by the use of 'yesterday', but has not correctly supplied the required form of the verb.

order of acquisition: See *developmental sequences.*

overgeneralization error: This type of error is the result of trying to use a rule in a context where it does not belong, for example, putting a regular *-ed* ending on an irregular verb, as in 'buyed' instead of 'bought'.

pattern practice drill: An audiolingual teaching technique in which learners are asked to practise sentences chosen to represent particular linguistic forms.

performance: The language that we actually use in listening, speaking, reading, writing. Performance is usually contrasted with *competence,* which is the knowledge which underlies our ability to use language. Performance is subject to variations due to inattention or fatigue whereas competence, at least for the mature native speaker, is more stable.

rate of development: The speed at which learners progress in their language development.

second language: Any language other than the first language learned. The abbreviation L2 is often used.

significant difference: This is a technical term which refers to differences between groups which, according to a variety of statistical tests, could not be due to chance. Such differences can be small or large. Their 'significance' is due to the consistency of the differences as well as its size.

simplification: Leaving out elements of a sentence, as when all verbs have the same form regardless of person, number, tense, for example, 'I go today. He go yesterday.'

structural grading: A technique for organizing or sequencing material in a textbook or lessons. The basis for the organization is a gradual increase in complexity of grammatical features.

substitution drill: An *audiolingual* teaching technique in which learners practise sentences, changing one element at a time, for example, 'I read a book'; 'I read a newspaper'; 'I read a story'.

subtractive bilingualism: The first language is partially or completely lost as a second language is acquired. This is often the result of learning a second language when one's first language skills are not fully developed.

target language: The language which is being learned, whether it is the first language or a second (or third or fourth) language.

task-based instruction: Instruction in which classroom activities are 'tasks' similar to those which learners might engage in outside the second or foreign language classroom. Tasks may be complex, for example, creating a school newspaper, or more limited, for example, making a phone call to reserve a train ticket.

teacher talk: See *modified input and foreigner talk.*

transfer: Learner's use of patterns of the first language in second language sentences. Also called 'interference'.

Universal Grammar (UG): Children's innate linguistic knowledge which, it is hypothesized consists of a set of principles common to all languages. This term has replaced the earlier term *language acquisition device* in work based on Chomsky's theory of language acquisition.

uptake: A learner's immediate response to corrective feedback on his/her utterances.

variational features: In contrast to the *developmental features* in the framework developed by Pienemann and his colleagues, variational features (for example, vocabulary, some grammatical morphemes) can be learned at any point in the learner's development.

zone of proximal development (ZPD): The level of performance which a learner is capable of when there is support from interaction with a more advanced interlocutor.

BIBLIOGRAPHY

This list of books and articles is not meant to be an exhaustive bibliography of the field of language learning. Rather, it brings together all the works which have been cited in this book as well as those which have been suggested for further reading.

Allwright, R. L. 1988. *Observation in the Language Classroom.* London: Longman.

Arenberg, L. 1987. *Raising Children Bilingually: The Pre-School Years.* Clevedon, Somerset: Multilingual Matters.

Asher, J. 1972. 'Children's first language as a model for second language learning.' *Modern Language Journal* 56/3: 133–9.

Baker, C. 1995. *A Parents' and Teachers' Guide to Bilingualism.* Clevedon, Somerset: Multilingual Matters.

Bardovi-Harlig, K. and **D. Reynolds.** 1995. 'The role of lexical aspect in the acquisition of tense and aspect.' *TESOL Quarterly* 29/1: 107–31.

Baron, N. 1992. *Growing Up with Language.* Reading, Mass.: Addison-Wesley.

Berko Gleason, J. 1989. *The Development of Language.* Columbus, Ohio: Merrill.

Bialystok, E. and **E. Ryan.** 1985. 'A metacognitive framework for the development of first and second language skills' in D. Forrest-Presley, G. Mackinnon, and T. Waller (eds.): *Metacognition, Cognition, and Human Performance,* vol. 12. New York: Academic Press, pp. 207–52.

Bloom, L., L. Hood, and **P. M. Lightbown.** 1974. 'Imitation in child language: If, when, and why.' *Cognitive Psychology* 6/3: 380–420. Reprinted in L. Bloom and M. Lahey (eds.). 1978. *Readings in Language Development.* New York: John Wiley.

Bloom, L. and **M. Lahey.** 1978. *Language Development and Language Disorders.* New York: John Wiley.

Brown, H. D. 1994. *Teaching by Principles: An Interactive Approach to Language Pedagogy.* Englewood Cliffs, N.J.: Prentice-Hall Regents.

Brown, R. 1973. *A First Language: The Early Stages.* Cambridge, Mass.: Harvard University Press.

Burstall, C. 1975. 'French in the primary school: The British experiment.' *Canadian Modern Language Review* 31/5: 388–402.

Chaudron, C. 1988. *Second Language Classrooms: Research on Teaching and Learning.* Cambridge: Cambridge University Press.

Chomsky, N. 1959. Review of *Verbal Behavior* by B. F. Skinner. *Language* 35/1: 26–58.

Chomsky, N. 1981. *Lectures on Government and Binding.* Dordrecht: Foris. Chapter 1.

Cook, V. 1988. *Chomsky's Universal Grammar.* London: Basil Blackwell.

Cook, V. 1991. *Second Language Learning and Language Teaching.* London: Edward Arnold.

Corder, S. P. 1967. 'The significance of learners' errors.' *International Review of Applied Linguistics* 5/2–3: 161–69.

Crago, M. 1992. 'Communicative interaction and second language acquisition: An Inuit example.' *TESOL Quarterly* 26/3: 487–505.

Crookes, G. and **Schmidt, R.** 1991. Motivation: 'Reopening the research agenda.' *Language Learning* 41/4: 469–512.

Cummins, J. 1984. *Bilingualism and Special Education: Issues in Assessment and Pedagogy.* Clevedon, Somerset: Multilingual Matters.

Curtiss, S. 1977. Genie: *A Psycholinguistic Study of a Modern-day 'Wild Child.'* New York: Academic Press.

Day, E. and **S. Shapson.** 1991. 'Integrating formal and functional approaches to language teaching in French immersion: An experimental approach.' *Language Learning* 41/1: 25–58.

Day, R. R. 1986. *Talking to Learn.* Rowley, Mass.: Newbury House.

de Villiers, J. G. and **P. A. de Villiers.** 1973. 'A cross-sectional study of the acquisition of grammatical morphemes.' *Journal of Psycholinguistic Research* 2/3: 267–78.

de Villiers, J. G. and **P. A. de Villiers.** 1978. *Language Acquisition.* Cambridge, Mass.: Harvard University Press.

Donato, R. 1994. 'Collective scaffolding in second language learning' in J. Lantolf and G. Appel (eds.): *Vygotskian Approaches to Second Language Research.* Norwood, N.J.: Ablex.

Döpke, S. 1992. *One Parent One Language: An Interactional Approach.* Amsterdam: John Benjamins.

Doughty, C. 1991. 'Second language instruction does make a difference: Evidence from an empirical study of SL relativization.' *Studies in Second Language Acquisition* 13/4: 431–69.

Doughty, C. and **J. Williams** (eds.). 1998. *Focus on Form in Classroom Second Language Acquisition.* Cambridge: Cambridge University Press.

Doughty, C. and **E. Varela.** 1997. 'Communicative focus on form' in C. Doughty and J. Williams (eds.): *Focus on Form in Classroom SLA.* Cambridge: Cambridge University Press.

Dulay, H., M. Burt and **S. Krashen.** 1982. *Language Two.* Oxford: Oxford University Press.

Eckman, F., L. Bell, and **D. Nelson.** 1988. 'On the generalization of relative clause instruction in the acquisition of English as a second language.' *Applied Linguistics* 9/1: 1–20.

Eimas, P., E. R. Siqueland, P. Jusczyk, and **J. Vigorito.** 1971. 'Speech perception in infants.' *Science* 171/3968: 303–6.

Ellis, N. C. and **R. Schmidt.** 1997. 'Morphology and longer distance dependencies.' *Studies in Second Language Acquisition* 19: 145–71.

Ellis, R. 1984. 'Can syntax be taught?' *Applied Linguistics* 5/2: 138–55.

Ellis, R. 1994. *The Study of Second Language Acquisition.* Oxford: Oxford University Press.

Ellis, R. 1997. *Second Language Acquisition.* Oxford: Oxford University Press.

Elman, J. L., E. A. Bates, M. H. Johnson, A. Karmiloff-Smith, D. Parisi, and **K. Plunkett.** 1996. *Rethinking Innateness: A Connectionist Perspective on Development.* Cambridge, Mass.: MIT Press.

Gardner, R. 1985. *Social Psychology and Second Language Learning: The Role of Attitudes and Motivation.* London: Edward Arnold.

Gardner, R. C. and **W. E. Lambert.** 1972. *Attitudes and Motivation in Second-Language Learning.* Rowley, Mass.: Newbury House.

Gass, S. 1982. 'From theory to practice' in M. Hines and W. Rutherford (eds.). *On TESOL '81.* Washington, D.C.: TESOL.

Gass, S. and **E. Varonis.** 1985. 'Task variation and nonnative/nonnative negotiation of meaning' in S. Gass and C. Madden (eds.): *Input in Second Language Acquisition.* Rowley, Mass.: Newbury House. pp. 149–61.

Gass, S. and **E. Varonis.** 1994. 'Input, interaction and second language production.' *Studies in Second Language Acquisition* 16/3: 283–302.

Gass, S., A. Mackey, and **T. Pica.** 1998. 'The role of input and interaction in second language acquisition: An introduction.' *Modern Language Journal* 82/3: 299–307.

Gass, S. M. and **J. Schachter** (eds.). 1989. *Linguistic Perspectives on Second Language Acquisition.* Cambridge: Cambridge University Press.

Gasser, M. 1990. 'Connectionism and universals of second language acquisition.' *Studies in Second Language Acquisition* 12: 179–99.

Genesee, F. 1976. 'The role of intelligence in second language learning.' *Language Learning* 26/2: 267–80.

Genesee, F. (ed.). 1995. *Educating Second Language Children: The Whole Child, the Whole Curriculum, the Whole Community.* Cambridge: Cambridge University Press.

Ginsburg, H. and S. Opper. 1969. *Piaget's Theory of Intellectual Development: An Introduction.* Englewood Cliffs, N.J.: Prentice-Hall.

Guiora, A., B. Beit-Hallahami, R. Brannon, C. Dull, and T. Scovel. 1972. 'The effects of experimentally induced changes in ego states on pronunciation ability in a second language: An exploratory study.' *Comprehensive Psychiatry* 13/5: 421–8.

Hamilton, R. 1994. 'Is implicational generalization unidirectional and maximal? Evidence from relativization instruction in a second language.' *Language Learning* 44/1: 123–57.

Hammerly, H. 1987. 'The immersion approach: Litmus test of second-language acquisition through classroom communication.' *Modern Language Journal* 71/4: 395–401.

Harley, B. 1989. 'Functional grammar in French immersion: A classroom experiment.' *Applied Linguistics* 10/3: 331–59.

Harley, B. 1993. 'Instructional strategies and SLA in early French immersion.' *Studies in Second Language Acquisition* 15/2: 245–59.

Harley, B. and M. Swain. 1984. 'The interlanguage of immersion students and its implications for second language teaching' in A. Davies, C. Criper, and A. Howatt (eds.): *Interlanguage.* Edinburgh: Edinburgh University Press. pp. 291–311.

Hatch, E. 1978. 'Discourse analysis and second language acquisition' in E. Hatch (ed.): *Second Language Acquisition: A Book of Readings.* Rowley, Mass.: Newbury House. pp. 401–35.

Hatch, E. 1992. *Discourse and Language Education.* Cambridge: Cambridge University Press.

Heath, S.B. 1983. *Ways with Words.* Cambridge: Cambridge University Press.

Higgs, T. V. and R. Clifford. 1982. 'The push toward communication' in T. V. Higgs (ed.): *Curriculum, Competence, and the Foreign Language Teacher.* Skokie, Ill.: National Textbook Co. pp. 57–79.

Ingram, D. 1989. *First Language Acquisition: Method, Description and Explanation.* Cambridge: Cambridge University Press.

Itard, J.-M.-G. 1962. *The Wild Boy of Aveyron (L'Enfant sauvage).* New York: Meredith.

Johnson, J., and E. Newport. 1989. 'Critical period effects in second language learning: The influence of maturational state on the acquisition of English as a Second Language.' *Cognitive Psychology* 21/1: 60–99.

Keenan, E. and **B. Comrie.** 1977. 'Noun phrase accessibility and Universal Grammar.' *Linguistic Inquiry* 8/1: 63–99.

Kellerman, E. 1986. 'An eye for an eye: Crosslinguistic constraints on the development of the L2 lexicon' in E. Kellerman and M. Sharwood Smith (eds.): *Crosslinguistic Influence in Second Language Acquisition.* New York: Pergamon.

Kowal, M. and **M. Swain.** 1994. 'Using collaborative language production tasks to promote students' language awareness.' *Language Awareness* 3/2: 73–91.

Krashen, S. 1982. *Principles and Practice in Second Language Acquisition.* Oxford: Pergamon.

Krashen, S. 1985. *The Input Hypothesis: Issues and Implications.* London: Longman.

Lado, R. 1964. *Language Teaching: A Scientific Approach.* New York: McGraw-Hill.

Lantolf, J. P., and **G. Appel.** 1994. *Vygotskian Approaches to Second Language Research.* Norwood, N.J.: Ablex.

Larsen-Freeman, D., and **M. H. Long.** 1991. *An Introduction to Second Language Acquisition.* New York: Longman.

Lenneberg, E. 1967. *The Biological Foundations of Language.* New York: John Wiley.

Lightbown, P. M. 1983. 'Acquiring English L2 in Quebec classrooms' in S. Felix and H. Wode (eds.): *Language Development at the Crossroads.* Tübingen: Gunter Narr. pp. 151–75.

Lightbown, P. M. 1985. 'Great expectations: Second language acquisition research and classroom teaching.' *Applied Linguistics* 6/2: 173–89.

Lightbown, P. M. 1987. 'Classroom language as input to second language acquisition' in C. Pfaff (ed.): *First and Second Language Acquisition Processes.* Cambridge, Mass.: Newbury House. pp. 169–87.

Lightbown, P. M. 1991. 'What have we here? Some observations on the role of instruction in second language acquisition' in R. Phillipson, E. Kellerman, L. Selinker, M. Sharwood Smith, and M. Swain (eds.): *Foreign/Second Language Pedagogy Research: A Commemorative Volume for Claus Færch.* Clevedon, Somerset: Multilingual Matters.

Lightbown, P. M. 1992. 'Can they do it themselves? A comprehension-based ESL course for young children' in R. Courchêne, J. Glidden, J. St. John, and C. Thérien (eds.): *Comprehension-based Second Language Teaching/L'Enseignement des langues secondes axé sur la compréhension.* Ottawa: University of Ottawa Press. pp. 353–70.

Lightbown, P. M. 1998. 'The importance of timing in focus on form' in C. Doughty and J. Williams (eds.): *Focus on Form in Classroom SLA,* Cambridge: Cambridge University Press.

Lightbown, P. M. and N. Spada. 1990. 'Focus on form and corrective feedback in communicative language teaching: Effects on second language learning.' *Studies in Second Language Acquisition* 12/4: 429–48.

Lightbown, P. M. and N. Spada. 1994. 'An innovative program for primary ESL in Quebec.' *TESOL Quarterly* 28/3: 563–79.

Long, M. 1980. 'Inside the "black box": Methodological issues in classroom research on language learning.' *Language Learning* 30/1: 1–42.

Long, M. H. 1983. 'Native speaker/non-native speaker conversation and the negotiation of comprehensible input.' *Applied Linguistics* 4: 126–41.

Long, M. H. 1985. 'Input and second language acquisition theory' in S. Gass and C. Madden (eds.): *Input in Second Language Acquisition*. Rowley, Mass.: Newbury House (pp. 377–93).

Long, M. H. 1990. 'Maturational constraints on language development.' *Studies in Second Language Acquisition* 12/3: 251–85.

Long, M. H. 1991. 'Focus on form: A design feature in language teaching methodology' in K. de Bot, D. Coste, R. Ginsberg, and C. Kramsch (eds.): *Foreign Language Research in Cross-cultural Perspective*. Amsterdam: John Benjamins. pp. 39–52.

Long, M. H., L. Adams, M. McLean, and F. Castanos. 1976. 'Doing things with words—verbal interaction in lockstep and small group classroom situations' in J. Faneslow and R. Crymes (eds.): *On TESOL '76*. Washington, D.C.: TESOL. pp. 137–53.

Long, M. and G. Crookes. 1992. 'Three approaches to task-based syllabus design.' *TESOL Quarterly* 26/1: 27–56.

Long, M. H. and P. Porter. 1985. 'Group work, interlanguage talk, and second language acquisition.' *TESOL Quarterly* 19/2: 207–28.

Lyster, R. 1994. 'The effect of functional–analytic teaching on aspects of French immersion students' sociolinguistic competence.' *Applied Linguistics* 15/3: 263–87.

Lyster, R. 1998. 'Recasts, repetition and ambiguity.' *Studies in Second Language Acquisition* 20/1: 51–81.

Lyster, R. and Ranta, L. 1997. 'Corrective feedback and learner uptake: Negotiation of form in communicative classrooms.' *Studies in Second Language Acquisition* 19/1, 37–61.

Mackey, A. 1999. 'Input, interaction and second language development: An empirical study of question formation in ESL.' *Studies in Second Language Acquisition* 21/4, 557–87.

Mackey, A. and J. Philp. 1998. 'Conversational interaction and second language development: Recasts, responses and Red Herrings.' *Modern Language Journal* 82/3: 338–56.

Malamah-Thomas, A. 1987. *Classroom Interaction.* Oxford: Oxford University Press.

McLaughlin, B. 1987. *Theories of Second Language Learning.* London: Edward Arnold.

Meisel, J. M. 1986. 'Reference to past events and actions in the development of natural second language acquisition' in C. Pfaff (ed.): *First and Second Language Acquisition Processes.* Cambridge, Mass.: Newbury House.

Meisel, J. M., H. Clahsen, and **M. Pienemann.** 1981. 'On determining developmental stages in natural second language acquisition.' *Studies in Second Language Acquisition* 3/2: 109–35.

Montgomery, C. and **M. Eisenstein.** 1985. 'Reality revisited: An experimental communicative course in ESL.' *TESOL Quarterly* 19/2: 317–34.

Naiman, N., M. Fröhlich, H. H. Stern, and **A. Todesco.** 1995. *The Good Language Learner.* Clevedon, UK: Multilingual Matters.

Newport, E. 1990. 'Maturational constraints on language learning.' *Cognitive Science* 14/1: 11–28.

Obler, L. 1989. 'Exceptional second language learners' in S. Gass, C. Madden, D. Preston, and L. Selinker (eds.): *Variation in Second Language Acquisition, Vol. II: Psycholinguistic Issues.* Clevedon, Somerset/Philadelphia, Pa.: Multilingual Matters. pp. 141–59.

Odlin, T. 1989. *Language Transfer.* Cambridge: Cambridge University Press.

Oxford, R. 1990. *Language Learning Strategies: What Every Teacher Should Know.* New York: Newbury House.

Oxford, R. and **J. Shearin.** 1994. 'Language learning motivation: Expanding the theoretical framework.' *Modern Language Journal* 78/1: 12–28.

Patkowski, M. 1980. 'The sensitive period for the acquisition of syntax in a second language.' *Language Learning* 30/2: 449–72.

Pica, T. 1994. 'Research on negotiation: What does it reveal about second language acquisition?' *Language Learning* 44: 493–527.

Pica, T., R. Young, and **C. Doughty.** 1987. 'The impact of interaction on comprehension.' *TESOL Quarterly* 21/4: 737–59.

Pienemann, M. 1985. 'Learnability and syllabus construction' in K. Hyltenstam and M. Pienemann (eds.): *Modelling and Assessing Second Language Acquisition.* Clevedon, Somerset: Multilingual Matters. pp. 23–75.

Pienemann, M. 1988. 'Determining the influence of instruction on L2 speech processing.' *AILA Review* 5/1: 40–72.

Pienemann, M. 1989. 'Is language teachable? Psycholinguistic experiments and hypotheses.' *Applied Linguistics* 10/1: 52–79.

Pienemann, M., M. Johnston, and **G. Brindley.** 1988. 'Constructing an acquisition-based procedure for second language assessment.' *Studies in Second Language Acquisition* 10/2: 217–43.

Pinker, S. 1994. *The Language Instinct.* New York: William Morrow.

Porter, P. 1986. 'How learners talk to each other: Input and interaction in task-centered discussions' in R. Day (ed.): *Talking to Learn: Conversation in Second Language Acquisition.* Rowley, Mass.: Newbury House.

Reid, J. 1987. 'The learning style preferences of ESL students.' *TESOL Quarterly* 21/1: 87–111.

Reid, J. (ed.) 1995. *Learning Styles in the ESL/EFL Classroom.* New York: Heinle and Heinle.

Richards, J. and **T. Rodgers.** 1986. *Approaches and Methods in Language Teaching.* Cambridge: Cambridge University Press.

Ringbom, H. 1986. 'Crosslinguistic influence and the foreign language learning process' in E. Kellerman and M. Sharwood Smith (eds.): *Crosslinguistic Influence in Second Language Acquisition.* New York: Pergamon Press.

Ritchie, W. C. and **T. K. Bhatia** (eds.). 1996. *Handbook of Second Language Acquisition.* San Diego, Cal.: Academic Press.

Rutherford, W. 1987. 'The meaning of grammatical consciousness-raising.' *World Englishes* 6/3: 209–16.

Rymer, R. 1993. *Genie: A Scientific Tragedy.* New York: HarperCollins.

Sachs, J., B. Bard, and **M. Johnson.** 1981. 'Language learning with restricted input: Case studies of two hearing children of deaf parents.' *Applied Psycholinguistics* 2/1: 33–54.

Saunders, G. 1988. *Bilingual Children: From Birth to Teens.* Clevedon, Somerset: Multilingual Matters.

Savignon, S. 1972. *Communicative Competence: An Experiment in Foreign-language Teaching.* Philadelphia, Pa.: Center for Curriculum Development.

Schachter, J. 1974. 'An error in error analysis.' *Language Learning* 24/2: 205–14.

Schieffelin, B. 1990. *The Give and Take of Everyday Life: Language Socialization of Kaluli Children.* Cambridge: Cambridge University Press.

Schieffelin, B. and **E. Ochs** (eds.). 1986. *Language Socialization Across Cultures.* Cambridge: Cambridge University Press.

Schmidt, R. 1990. 'The role of consciousness in second language learning.' *Applied Linguistics* 11: 17–46.

Schumann, J. 1979. 'The acquisition of English negation by speakers of Spanish: a review of the literature' in R. W. Andersen (ed.): *The Acquisition and Use of Spanish and English as First and Second Languages.* Washington, D.C.: TESOL.

Schwartz, B. 1993. 'On explicit and negative data effecting and affecting competence and linguistic behavior.' *Studies in Second Language Acquisition* 15: 147–163.

Scovel, T. 1988. *A Time to Speak: A Psycholinguistic Inquiry into the Critical Period for Human Speech*. Cambridge, Mass.: Newbury House.

Selinker, L. 1972. 'Interlanguage.' *IRAL* 10/2: 209–31.

Sharwood Smith, M. 1991. 'Speaking to many minds: On the relevance of different types of language information for the L2 learner.' *Second Language Research* 7/2: 118–32.

Sharwood Smith, M. 1993. 'Input enhancement in instructed SLA: Theoretical bases.' *Studies in Second Language Acquisition*, 15/2: 165–79.

Skehan, P. 1989. *Individual Differences in Second Language Learning*. London: Edward Arnold.

Skehan, P. 1991. 'Individual differences in second language learning.' *Studies in Second Language Acquisition* 13/2: 275–98.

Snow, C. E. and A. Ferguson (eds.). 1977. *Talking to Children: Language Input and Acquisition*. Cambridge: Cambridge University Press.

Snow, C. and M. Hoefnagel-Höhle. 1978. 'The critical period for language acquisition: Evidence from second language learning.' *Child Development* 49/4: 1114–28.

Spada, N. 1987. 'Relationships between instructional differences and learning outcomes: A process-product study of communicative language teaching.' *Applied Linguistics* 8/2: 137–61.

Spada, N. and M. Fröhlich. 1995. *The Communicative Orientation of Language Teaching Observation Scheme: Coding Conventions and Applications*. Sydney: National Centre for English Language Teaching and Research, Macquarie University.

Spada, N. and P. M. Lightbown. 1989. 'Intensive ESL programs in Quebec primary schools.' *TESL Canada Journal* 7/1: 11–32.

Spada, N. and P. M. Lightbown. 1993. 'Instruction and the development of questions in L2 classrooms.' *Studies in Second Language Acquisition* 15/2: 205–24.

Spada, N. and P. M. Lightbown. 1999. 'Instruction, L1 influence and developmental readiness in second language acquisition.' *Modern Language Journal* 83/1.

Swain, M. 1985. 'Communicative competence: Some roles of comprehensible input and comprehensible output in its development' in S. Gass and C. Madden (eds.): *Input in Second Language Acquisition*. Rowley, Mass.: Newbury House.

Swain, M. 1988. 'Manipulating and complementing content teaching to maximize second language learning.' *TESL Canada Journal* 6/1: 68–83.

Trahey, M. and **L.White.** 1993 'Positive evidence and preemption in the second language classroom.' *Studies in Second Language Acquisition* 15/2: 181–204.

VanPatten, B. and **T. Cadierno.** 1993. 'Explicit instruction and input processing.' *Studies in Second Language Acquisition* 15/2: 225–41.

VanPatten, B. and **C. Sanz.** 1995. 'From input to output: Processing instruction and communicative tasks' in F. Eckman, D. Highland, P. Lee, J. Mileham and R. Weber (eds.): *Second Language Acquisition: Theory and Pedagogy.* Mahwah, NJ: Lawrence Erlbaum Associates.

Vygotsky, L. S. 1978. *Mind in Society.* Cambridge, Mass.: Harvard University Press.

Wajnryb, R. 1990. *Grammar Dictation.* Oxford: Oxford University Press.

Wajnryb, R. 1992. *Classroom Observation Tasks: A Resource Book for Language Teachers and Trainers.* Cambridge: Cambridge University Press.

Wertsch, J. V. 1985. *Vygotsky and the Social Formation of Mind.* Cambridge, Mass.: Harvard University Press.

Wesche, M. B. 1981. 'Language aptitude measures in streaming, matching students with methods, and diagnosis of learning problems' in K. Diller (ed.): *Individual Differences and Universals in Language Learning Aptitude.* Rowley, Mass.: Newbury House. pp. 119–39.

White, J. 1998. 'Getting the learners' attention: A typographical input enhancement study' in C. Doughty and J. Williams (eds.): *Focus on Form in Classroom SLA.* Cambridge: Cambridge University Press.

White, L. 1987. 'Against comprehensible input: The input hypothesis and the development of second-language competence.' *Applied Linguistics* 8/2: 95–110.

White, L. 1989. *Universal Grammar and Second Language Acquisition.* Amsterdam/Philadelphia, Pa.: John Benjamins.

White, L. 1991. 'Adverb placement in second language acquisition: some effects of positive and negative evidence in the classroom.' *Second Language Research* 7/2: 133–61.

White, L., N. Spada, P. M. Lightbown, and **L. Ranta.** 1991. 'Input enhancement and syntactic accuracy in L2 acquisition.' *Applied Linguistics* 12/4: 416–32.

Wong-Fillmore, L. 1991. 'When learning a second language means losing the first.' *Early Childhood Research Quarterly* 6/3: 323–46.

Yorio, C. 1986. 'Consumerism in second language learning and teaching.' *Canadian Modern Language Review* 42/3: 668–87.

Yule, G. and **D. Macdonald.** 1990. 'Resolving referential conflicts in L2 interaction: The effect of proficiency and interactive role.' *Language Learning* 40/4: 539–56.

Zobl, H. 1982. 'A direction for contrastive analysis: The comparative study of developmental sequences.' *TESOL Quarterly* 16/2: 169–83.

INDEX

Entries relate to Chapters 1 to 7 and the glossary. References to the glossary are indicated by 'g' after the page number.